Praise for *The Warrior* 

D0393627

"Irresistible, engaging, and liberating in a way that only the truth can. A much-needed guide to moving beyond the chatter of the mind and the noise of the emotions to discovering true peace."

—Alberto Villoldo, Ph.D., author of *One Spirit Medicine* and *Shaman, Healer, Sage*

"*The Warrior Heart Practice* is an inner journey toward inner healing and peace, through feeling, story, truth, and intent—the Four Chambers of the Warrior Heart. This book is a reflection of a warrior putting into practice all that she has learned, the moment when knowledge turns into wisdom, in order to heal a heart that is not afraid to love."

—Don Miguel Ruiz Jr, author of *The Mastery of Self* and *The Five Levels of Attachment*

"HeatherAsh Amara has the amazing gift of identifying key issues that are critical for us to look at in order to experience our authentic self, our truth, and to feel empowered. The Warrior Heart is filled with a wealth of tools to perform an inner clearing of old stories, release agreements that limit us, and leave us feeling stuck and disconnected from our creative strength. HeatherAsh Amara is a brilliant guide!"

—Sandra Ingerman, M.A., award-winning author of twelve books, including *Soul Retrieval* and *The Book of Ceremony: Shamanic Wisdom for Invoking the Sacred into Everyday Life*

"HeatherAsh Amara is a trustworthy and seasoned guide, helping us discover the unexplored regions of our hearts. She gets us to the real questions, leading us towards lives that agree with our deepest convictions. The Warrior Heart Practice is an invaluable resource for finding out what we really want and who we really are."

—Clark Strand and Perdita Finn, authors of
*The Way of the Rose: The Radical Path of the Divine
Feminine Hidden in the Rosary*

"HeatherAsh takes readers on a journey to truly heal our minds and emotions. The Warrior Heart Practice is a powerful inquiry practice that will help anyone, from business people to athletes, from parents to those working through trauma or abuse, and from those in recovery or in big life transition to claim their courage and power and step into their most authentic self."

—Dannion Brinkley, author of *Saved by the Light*

"HeatherAsh Amara arouses us to step out of our little stories into a bigger and braver story. She guides us, chamber by chamber, through the practice of finding and following the truth of the heart. She inspires us to be artists of life and wide-awake dreamers who can manifest what we most deeply desire when we move beyond ego agendas, follow the secret wishes or our souls, and recruit the wisdom of the body and the blessing of a greater self."

—Robert Moss, bestselling author of *Conscious Dreaming, The
Secret History of Dreaming,* and *Dreaming the Soul Back Home*

"In this wonderfully helpful and enlightening book, HeatherAsh Amara tells us that 'in each moment we have the choice to wake up, reconnect to our inner light, and stop believing the stories and lies our minds tells us.' Drawing from personal stories and deep wells of Toltec wisdom, HeatherAsh has produced a masterpiece of a guidebook to show us the way to transformation."

—Beverly Donfrio, author of *Riding in Cars with
Boys* and *Astonished*

"Welcome to the evolution of wisdom! The Warrior Heart Practice is a compassionate, stunningly practical technique for self-discovery and transformation in any situation. HeatherAsh Amara is one of our most gifted and authentic spiritual teachers and her simple elegant process instantly helps us access and embody the deep insight within us all."

—Irene O'Garden, award-winning poet,
playwright, and author of *Risking the Rapids*

"This is a restorative book, full of the sort of wisdom and honesty that transforms life. HeatherAsh Amara shares her own story in a way that gives her the credibility as a teacher and reveals how her own extraordinary quest for healing and joy is universal."

—Jacob Nordby, author of *Blessed Are the Weird—
A Manifesto for Creatives*

"By walking bravely with open hearts through the Four Chambers, we navigate the turbulent waters of life to overcome depression, alienation, and wounding. We emerge empowered with the warrior's heart energy to become a beacon of light in our world."

—Luisah Teish, author of *Jambalaya: The Natural Woman's Book of
Personal Charms and Practical Rituals*

"In *Warrior Heart*, HeatherAsh tackles the murky landscape where personal experience mingles with external facts, and guides us beyond the repetitive stories that no longer serve us to absolute freedom."

—Chantal Pierrat, CEO, Emerging Women

ALSO BY HEATHERASH AMARA

*Warrior Goddess Training:*
*Become the Woman You Are Meant to Be*

*The Seven Secrets of Happy and Healthy Relationships*
(with don Miguel Ruiz Jr.)

# The
# *Warrior Heart Practice*

### A Simple Process to
### Transform Confusion into Clarity
### and Pain into Peace

. . .

## HeatherAsh Amara

ST. MARTIN'S
**ESSENTIALS**
NEW YORK

*To all the warriors of the heart who walked before us,*
*shining the light of their courage and love*
*for the rest of us to follow*

The information in this book is not intended to replace the advice of the reader's own physician or other medical professional. You should consult a medical professional in matters relating to health, especially if you have existing medical conditions, and before starting, stopping, or changing the dose of any medication you are taking. Individual readers are solely responsible for their own health-care decisions. The author and the publisher do not accept responsibility for any adverse effects individuals may claim to experience, whether directly or indirectly, from the information contained in this book.

First published in the United States by St. Martin's Essentials,
an imprint of St. Martin's Publishing Group

THE WARRIOR HEART PRACTICE. Copyright © 2020 by HeatherAsh Amara.
All rights reserved. Printed in the United States of America. For information, address
St. Martin's Publishing Group, 120 Broadway, New York, NY 10271.

www.stmartins.com

Graphics by Kevin Anthony Flores

The Library of Congress Cataloging-in-Publication Data is available upon request.

ISBN 978-1-250-23058-4 (trade paperback)
ISBN 978-1-250-23059-1 (ebook)

Our books may be purchased in bulk for promotional, education, or business use.
Please contact your local bookseller or the Macmillan Corporate and Premium
Sales Department at 1-800-221-7945, extension 5442, or by email at
MacmillanSpecialMarkets@macmillan.com

First Edition: January 2020

10   9   8   7   6   5   4   3   2   1

# Contents

# Preface

This book emerged from the seeds of need, frustration, and love.

One day, as I was having lunch with one of my best friends, he began sharing his story of pain, self-doubt, and fear, which he repeatedly shared with anyone who was willing to listen. The repetitive voices inside his head were harsh, and he couldn't get away from them. The cycle was deeply entrenched, and I found myself moving toward that edge where I would no longer be able to hold space for him.

As he told me about the experience he couldn't let go of, I reflected his perspective of it back to him in an effort to show him how skewed his version of the story was. I would listen and say, "Fred, that's actually not a true story, because I was there. This is what *actually* happened." And he'd say, "You're right! That is what happened! Okay!" And then he'd get totally solid again. He'd have an aha moment that allowed him to see more clearly, feel better, and leave his story behind, which then enabled him to go about his day.

A few days later, he would come to me with the exact same story, spoken with the same amount of angst and self-punishment, as if he had never shared it with anyone before.

We've all had stories like this that snag the fabric of our being, where an experience gets caught, but rather than reflect and challenge the story, we keep going back again and again to pick at the loose stitch. Whether the experience happened in childhood or yesterday, our stories can unravel our self-esteem, drain our energy, and keep us struggling in emotional quicksand.

As I looked at my friend, I could see the pain in his face, his closure, and his self-hatred. Despite repeated attempts to pull him out from under the drowning heaviness of his story, nothing was working. So I offered up a prayer: "Please let me help my friend see and hold the truth."

As I opened my heart to his suffering, I felt an entire process of getting to the truth drop into my being, and right then and there, a practice that I call the *Warrior Heart* was born.

Since that day, I've been teaching, practicing, and sharpening the tools of the Warrior Heart practice. It is a straightforward and well-tested system that will help you untangle your emotions from your stories and your stories from the truth, then connect the truth with your intent. This systematic exploration toward truth is an inquiry practice using Toltec wisdom as the framework and your emotional body as a starting point.

In *The Warrior Heart Practice*, you will learn how to move through a simple process that transforms confusion into clarity and pain into peace.

Feeling, Story, Truth, Intent: These are the four chambers of the Warrior Heart practice, which change the way you operate in the world by helping you to rearrange the pieces of your personal puzzles into an integrated new whole—mentally, emotionally, and physically.

I wrote this book because I am passionate about helping humans get free from the inside out. I've watched myself and so many of my friends, peers, and students struggle with self-worth, fear of rejection, self-doubt, shame, and blame. For way too many of us, our precious attention and energy are consumed every day just by trying to manage our judgmental mind and our emotional reactions.

We are amazing, creative, powerful creatures, and instead of waking up each day saying, "What beauty and connection will I craft today?" we wake up basically saying, "How can I feel good enough about myself today?" or "How can I avoid my own self-judgment and fears?" The vitality that could be going toward solving world problems, bringing people together in wondrous ways, and celebrating the unbelievably great gift of life is instead drained by drama, conflict, and using the power of our words against ourselves.

The Warrior Heart practice will teach you numerous ways to ascertain the ofttimes subtle or hard-to-see differences between the truth and a story. In plain terms: Through this process, you will learn how to stop the drain and misery of suffering and self-limitation and start creatively living your best life. You'll also learn the importance and skill of how to harness your individual intent and allow the power of Intent, or Life, to move through you.

The first two chapters are the "map" section of the book: a big-picture overview of where we are and where we are going. Remember in the olden days, before GPS and cell phones, when we had these huge things called *paper maps*? If you were lost, the first thing you would do was unfold your map and figure out where you were. Then you would look to find where you were going. Just as if we are on a journey together, in *The Warrior Heart Practice* we will start by mapping out where we are as humans and where we are going.

The remaining chapters are the "method," the nuts and bolts of how we travel the road from where we are to where we are going. With deep compassion for the often-bumpy road of human experience, I'll guide you through a specific practice for releasing denial, shame, and resistance while also helping you align with your innate kick-ass authenticity. You'll learn how to follow or deepen your relationship with the wise guidance within; shed fear, anxiety, and self-loathing; and come back in touch with your potent mental, emotional, and physical wisdom.

As you move through the four chambers in *The Warrior Heart Practice*, you will rekindle the power of deep intimacy with self; release self-judgment, guilt, and shame; and claim the path of being an aware, transformative Warrior of the Heart. Chapters range from serious to playful, with a fearless approach toward difficult subjects you may be facing, such as loss, difficult relationships, or addiction.

## *Your Inner Beacon of Light*

No matter how much you have suffered or how much you suffer now, whether you feel slightly dissatisfied or completely lost and confused, there is a light illuminating your way if you only look for it with new eyes. The purpose of this book is to remind you that a beacon of light constantly shines within you like a lighthouse on the coast, guiding you away from the familiar but rocky shores of struggle, stress, and suffering, and showing you the way toward the true harbor of your innate integrity and peace.

The current waters in which we live are turbulent, unpredictable, and filled with fears of not being or doing "enough." If you suffer from a troubling lack of confidence and a bounty of self-judgment despite your successes, if you feel unfulfilled in your relationships or work, or if you have a nagging sense that there is something vital missing within, then you are living within the shallow waters of who you think you are supposed to be rather than from the nourishing depth of who you truly are.

While the pure light of your being is always shining, it can and does get buried beneath years of trying to please other people, an accumulation of hurts, and life's daily demands. Silence underlies all sound, whether it is a whisper or a pounding wave. In the middle of a raging storm, the underlying stillness is overwhelmed, but it is still there, ready to be accessed at any time. Beneath the choppy waves of your mind and the crashing loudness of fearful emotions lie the silent depths of your authentic expression.

*The Warrior Heart Practice* shares a pathway to support you in moving beneath your mental and emotional noise so that you can immerse yourself in the inspiration and stillness within you. This book will show you how to move beyond the struggles of everyday life where we often seek outside approval, and how to be less serious and more ecstatic on your healing, work, or spiritual path. It offers tools for finding ease and flow rather than struggle in your relationships and how to be more grounded, present, and playful.

The question is not "Is it really possible to live from my authenticity and heart?" but rather "How do I free myself from the mental prison of judgment, comparison, self-criticism, and worry to create a life built on true acceptance, unshakable inner joy, and bountiful trust? How do I find and sustain connection to the profound creative brilliance and capacity that lie within the core of my being?"

The truth is you are a magnificent, nuclear bomb force of love and potential. And if you've had enough of playing small and judging yourself into scattered, itty-bitty pieces of who you really are, this book will awaken the warrior within that you need to claim who you are really meant to be.

This book is a bridge and the cleansing waters flowing beneath it simultaneously. The Warrior Heart's big-picture view will help you accept and integrate all the parts of you so that you are once again connected to your creative, inspired inner wisdom. The specific method of the Warrior Heart practice is like a power washer that will wash away the debris that has accumulated and clouded your authentic knowing.

Within these pages, you will learn how to celebrate both your divine nature and your quirky personality, while balancing practical action with spiritual inspiration.

I'm excited to be on this journey with you.

To get the most out of this book, I recommend that you read each of the chapters, getting an overview of the teachings and the different chambers. Skip over the exercises and questions for later. Then come back and review each chapter, adding in the exercises and questions. You don't have to do every exercise; you may start out by doing one per chapter or picking the exercises or questions that most speak to you.

If you are ready to jump in and want to go deep quickly, make sure you have a journal specifically for the Warrior Heart practice. Read chapter I, answer the questions at the end of the chapter, and then print out several of the Warrior Heart practice sheets at the end of chapter 2 that you can use for specific issues as they arise. At the end of each chapter, review and answer the questions, and do each of the exercises.

The Warrior Heart practice is a simple sequential process; through the coming chapters, I will take you step-by-step through how to find your truth and view your story in a totally different way. While there is no right way to use the book, I do recommend that you get to know each of the different chambers and do them in order as you learn the practice. Then as you get more adept, you can begin to improvise and use the chambers in a way that best serves where you are.

Before we get into the map and method of the practice, let me introduce myself, and how the Warrior Heart teachings came to be.

# Introduction

In 1973, my parents brought my sister and me to India. We went as tourists with the intent of touching the luminous beauty of the Taj Mahal and to be touched by the immense contrasts of poverty, chaos, devotion, and peace that pervade India. I was seven years old.

Earlier that year, I had decided to write a book, but when I sat down to start my bestseller, a sudden insight gave me pause. Sitting there at my wooden desk with my pad of lavender paper and my favorite black felt-tip pen in hand, I realized I was missing one crucial ingredient to be an author:

Experience.

So I put away my paper and pen and went outside to play. I trusted implicitly that what I needed to write for my book would come. Many experiences, which I would eventually write about, began a few months later with a life-altering, four-second event.

The catalyst for this awakening came wrapped in the package of an Indian child who was about my age. I saw her as I was walking down a dusty New Delhi street while I was holding my dad's hand. I remember the heavy, sticky heat, looking down, and worrying that my white sandals were going to get dirty. When I looked back up, I suddenly locked eyes with this young Indian girl walking toward me.

She was barefoot, draped in a soiled fragment of a dress that wrapped around an all-elbows-and-knees frame. I almost looked away, embarrassed by my clean dress, shiny shoes, and full belly. But as we came closer, our gaze became even more connected. Everything around me stopped. The noise of the traffic dissolved. The fear I hadn't realized I was holding simply evaporated. As I looked deeply into her brown eyes, a warm sun radiated out from her heart. Every cell in my being smiled in utter happiness, and as this occurred, she reflected the same utter happiness and recognition in her smile back to me.

I felt as if I had reunited with my best friend after many long years of separation. This feeling did not dissolve after she had passed; it only grew stronger. I was ecstatic. I felt like I'd been dipped in liquid beauty. Everything around me became a sweet song that I suddenly remembered how to sing.

What I learned in that seconds-long merging, which I've forgotten and re-remembered many times since that day, is that within each of us resides a clear pool of peace and an unbreakable core connection, regardless of our circumstances. The state I felt in those four seconds was the awakening of my authentic Warrior Heart.

Authenticity is the state of being undivided, in integrity, and clear. When we are in wholeness, we are rooted in our truest nature, and we live our lives from a conscious and clear place of faith in ourselves and the wisdom of our Warrior Heart. We learn to navigate our challenges with more and more grace, faith, and presence.

Like my experience with the girl in India, all of us have those precious moments or days of connection and openhearted abiding love for life. We touch this state when we fall in love, hold a baby, or achieve a longtime goal. But when our happiness or self-worth is tied to a moment, person, or place rather than anchored in our being as our authentic Warrior Heart expression, it is frustratingly fleeting and transitory. It takes tools and practice to stabilize this state of inner joy that is independent from our external experience. Here is how I discovered the raw materials and my own inner fire to forge a new, healthy, stable, and fiercely engaged relationship between myself and life.

## The Toltec Tradition

From the moment I put my childhood pen down to go out and play and gain more experience, I've been blessed with an abundance of adventures. I've traveled around the world many times over, studied with different spiritual teachers and healers, and eagerly searched for and welcomed connection and meaning.

In the early 1990s, I dreamed that I would soon meet a person who would change the course of my life. A few weeks later, a friend excitedly told me about a teacher from the Toltec tradition who was visiting our area. I had no idea what a *Toltec* was, but when I heard don Miguel's name, it struck a familiar chord deep within my body that rang like a bell struck at dawn. I felt a full-body knowing and that same liquid beauty that I had felt as a child. This knowing vibrated through me when I met the Toltec community and especially when I first heard don Miguel speak. I knew I had come home.

The word *Toltec* means "artist of the spirit," and the Toltec path is one of personal freedom—the freedom to choose how we want to create our inner and outer world through our perceptions and intent. Many people in the 1970s and 1980s were first introduced to Toltec philosophy through the writings of Carlos Castaneda as he shared his experiences with Yaqui Indian don Juan Matus. In the late 1990s, don Miguel Ruiz's first book, *The Four Agreements,* opened a new and understandable pathway to access this ancient tradition. While Castaneda's writings were like a lightning bolt that illuminated a radical new way of being, Ruiz's book was a trusty flashlight that shined a clear path to releasing personal suffering and reclaiming our natural state: happiness.

"The real mission you have in life," don Miguel writes, "is to make yourself happy, and in order to be happy you have to look at what you believe, the way you judge yourself, and the way you victimize yourself." Prior to immersing myself in the Toltec teachings, I would have said I was happy. I had work I enjoyed, a partner whom I loved, and a great community surrounding me. On the surface, I *was* happy. But deep inside, I struggled with feeling flawed, with the constant fear of not being good enough, and with deep-seated self-criticism. When I embraced the Toltec teachings and dove deeply into exploring myself, I discovered an eternal connected wisdom flowing within and around me.

For six years, I participated in an intense apprenticeship with don Miguel and traveled the world with him. While on these journeys, I was doing the work of untangling my old belief system, which was built on judgment and victimization. I was learning to re-create myself from the inside out. I learned to see myself not as someone who was broken and needed to be fixed but as a powerful woman with the capacity to reclaim my energy from old patterns and habits. I traded in trying to be perfect for playfully embracing all of me. I swapped out taking things personally and caretaking for gratitude in knowing that it is everyone's right to dream the dream they wanted. With this awareness, I gave away needing to be right or fix others and chose to discover my own inner gifts and resources.

At the heart of the Toltec path to presence and authenticity is recognizing that we are all dreamers creating reality through our thoughts and actions. In each moment, we have the choice to wake up, reconnect to our inner light, and stop believing the stories and lies our mind tells us.

As artists of spirit, Toltecs consciously re-create the dream of their life into one of beauty. "If you can see yourself as an artist, and you can see that your life is your own creation, then why not create the most beautiful story possible for yourself?" (don Miguel, *The Four Agreements*) He goes on to say, "Find yourself and express yourself in your own particular way. Express your love openly. Life is nothing but a dream, and if you create your life with love, your dream becomes a masterpiece of art."

While I still felt like a novice at creating my life as a masterpiece of art, I was soon given a much bigger canvas to paint my dreams on.

## Becoming My Own Artist

In 1999, don Miguel gave me a huge boost on my path to becoming my own artist, one of those gifts that at the time felt more like a punishment than a treat.

In the inner sanctum of a cool, dark-gray stone temple in Egypt, surrounded by his top teachers, don Miguel announced that he was disbanding our circle. "Go make the teachings your own," he told us. "I am no longer your teacher." I was in a state of shock. I stayed in the temple with my friend Gini long after everyone else had left. I was now a freed bird not yet trusting my ability to fly or knowing what direction I needed to go. In the following fifteen years, I started teaching full-time, opened up Toltec centers in Berkeley and then Austin, and digested everything I had learned from don Miguel to incorporate with my other, now plentiful, life experiences.

While the writings in *The Warrior Heart Practice* are founded in the Eagle Knight lineage of don Miguel Ruiz, I've also gathered and integrated wisdom from every Toltec book in print, along with my own inner unfolding. The resources for this book span from the teachings of Toltec grandfather don Juan via Carlos Castaneda to the writings of many apprentices of don Juan, don Miguel, and other Toltec authors.

Early in my training, don Miguel introduced what he called *the Toltec cosmology* to a group of apprentices. I recall frantically taking notes as I had wave after wave of understanding and clarity about my purpose and next steps. And so it began. The Toltec cosmology is an energetic model of the spiritual and physical experience of humans. To this day, it continues to be the most illuminating synopsis of human development I've ever come across. This model forms the eagle's-eye perspective for *The Warrior Heart Practice.*

Here's a very abbreviated look at the Toltec cosmology's big-picture view.

From the Toltec perspective, every human contains a unique ray of light that is his or her individual manifestation of spirit in form. This eternal part of us, or what we call our *Big Soul,* remembers its connection to source and all of life. It does not see itself as different or special but as one facet of a multifaceted, divinely radiant jewel. This was the energy I tapped when

I connected with the Indian girl, which is a state of being we have access to all the time if we only turn to face and receive it.

But there is a reason it can be so difficult to remember this peaceful place within, what we call *ego-personality*, or Little Soul. This part of us believes we are separate and will actually fight to stay alone, aloof, and miserable.

In the next chapter, we will explore the importance of re-connecting your Little Soul to your Big Soul and the power of learning to connect with the vastness of your Big Soul as much as you accept and support your quirky, scared, and often stubborn ego-personality.

# 1

# Remembering the Connection

*We don't realize that, somewhere within us all, there does*
*exist a supreme self who is eternally at peace.*

—Elizabeth Gilbert

Remember, forget. remember, forget. Remember, forget. I used to be so frustrated with myself. I would have an insight or aha moment and come back to myself and my experience and heart, then soon enough forget who I was and be once again pulled back into who I thought people wanted me to be or who I had been in the past. Aaargh!

This cycle of losing myself and finding myself felt like a kind of slow torture. Plus, it was exhausting. One moment, I would feel centered and happily aligned with my life, and the next moment, something would happen—an old memory, a run-in with a boss or friend, a bounced check or late report—and my self-esteem and happiness would be splattered on the ground like broken eggs dropped from a roof.

I could see that my core beliefs of wanting others to like me, my desire to control people and things, and my seeking of attention and approval from the outside kept derailing my life. But I felt helpless to change it. I didn't understand the mechanics of how I could have glimpses of joyful wholeness and then so thoroughly forget and plunge into struggle, shame, or fear.

Oftentimes, we lose our way and no longer recognize the ever-present bond that lovingly connects the parts of who we are. As I discovered through years of remembering and forgetting and then finally embodying a new way, there is a powerful Warrior Heart inside all of us where our spirit (or Big Soul) and our mental, emotional, and physical being are connected and on our team, rather than feeling like bickering enemies.

In this chapter, we'll look at what has happened that made us forget this inner connection and why it is so important to reconnect our ego-personality to our Big Soul. Afterward, we'll take a look at a new way of viewing your whole self—one that will create space for change to happen more rapidly.

Let's take a look at the difference between living from the radiance of your true nature and living from the exhaustion of drama, self-judgment, and fear. Once you have the big-picture overview of where you are right now, as well as where you are headed, the four chambers of the Warrior Heart practice will be your guide to staying on the path.

## Big Soul and Little Soul

As a human, you are the perfect blend of ethereal and physical: half spirit and half animal. Your spiritual Big Soul always remembers its vastness and creative nature, while your animal self focuses on survival, safety, and (hopefully) the pleasures of the physical body. Your physical form is a brilliant anchor that allows your spirit to explore, experience, and enjoy this earthly plane. This creative union of you as spirit and matter is precious and unique—and can be seriously fun!

Or it can be a nightmare of painful experiences and broken dreams.

When you were very young, you naturally lived from your Big Soul merged with your physical form and experienced everything in life as a force of which you were an integral part. You engaged fully in the delight of all your senses. Your spiritual Big Soul and your physical being were like two best friends, hand in hand, playfully exploring a vast and exciting new world.

The Toltec view describes the split that often happens between these two allies as we grow. For some of us, this split happens very early on, even when we are babies or before we have language. For others, the split happens later, often when we learn language and begin creating separation from the world around us. This cosmological model—which I have spent many years studying, exploring, and teaching—is like a global satellite map of the human experience. Below is a simplified version of this model, which is designed to help guide you back into your Warrior Heart by illustrating the importance of reuniting your Big Soul and your ego-personality (Little Soul) as long-lost friends rather than as the strangers (or even enemies) they have become.

Your relationship to your Little Soul, and whether it is connected or disconnected from your Big Soul, is the crucial factor for whether your life is filled with struggle and separation or with joyful ease and a sense of wholeness. When your Little Soul and your Big Soul are allied, you flourish in the delight of your own integrity, your own wholeness.

Do you remember what it was like to live joyfully, filled with child-awe and dedicated to playful exploration—or have you watched young kids do so? You can have that same love of life, resiliency, and enthusiasm as an adult too. It's just a matter of learning how to reconnect. Let's take a look at how the split occurs between Big Soul and your Little Soul so that the path back to your natural state is clear.

The diagrams in the following pages are simplified snapshots of the Toltec cosmology. As you look at them, feel within you what they represent and how they relate to your own experience of remembering and forgetting.

At the center is your Big Soul, bright like the sun and radiating out rays of "Yes! We are one boundless being of energy and spirit! How shall we explore in this wonderful physical/ mental/emotional package?!" The physical/mental/emotional being is represented in this drawing by a circle that surrounds the central point of your Big Soul.

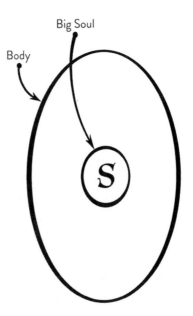

Big Soul

Body

Your Little Soul is represented by a dot on the edge of the circle of your physical/mental/emotional being. When you are a child, the rays of your Big Soul fill this circle, infusing your physical, mental, and emotional being and your ego-personality—or sense of *I*—with joyful curiosity. Again, your Little Soul is important: This is your separate sense of self and your quirky, unique personality.

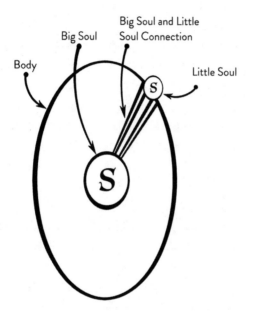

But when our Little Soul loses its way and grasps onto fearful thoughts (such as *I'm not good enough, I need to be perfect,* or *Bad things are going to happen to me or to the ones I love*), it becomes more and more difficult to hear the loving voice of our Big Soul. For most adults, the circle of our physical/mental/emotional self has become filled with fears and judgments that obscure the light of our inner sun.

The once-seamless connection between our spiritual nature

and our physical form is torn. Instead of making choices from the wisdom of our bountiful Big Soul allied with our ego-personality, we begin to identify more and more with the Little Soul thoughts of who we "should" be rather than the Big Soul–Little Soul union of who we truly are.

In his book *A New Earth*, Eckhart Tolle describes our ego as an "illusory sense of self" based on unconscious identification with our memories and thoughts. This identification creates what Tolle calls our *pain-body*, an accumulation of old emotional pain. In *The Four Agreements*, don Miguel calls the Little Soul a *parasite*, because for most adults, our ego-personality has split from our Big Soul and now feeds on the energy of fear. Tolle and don Miguel are using different words, but they are describing the same concept: the separation of our Little Soul from our Big Soul.

I see the Little Soul as a small child. When a child is intimately connected to a loving, wise, nurturing caretaker (Big Soul), it is fun to go out and explore the world and then come back and share what it has learned. If a child discovers something scary or confusing during her explorations and then comes back to check in with her older and wiser best friend, Big Soul reminds her of the big picture by showing her that she is part of something vast and wonderful. Once reassured, the child smiles and goes off to play again, realizing that she is engaging in a fabulous dream that she is cocreating. The child thus gains experiences and matures from a base of unconditional love and security. This is, of course, the ideal situation, but many of us do not even know that this is possible.

Now imagine what would happen if that child went out to play and lost her way back to Big Soul, her best friend and wise guide. Can you imagine yourself as a little kid lost in a busy outdoor marketplace? How would you feel? What would you do? Take a moment to imagine that sense of being lost and of believing that you have to figure out how to stay safe in a seemingly unfriendly, unfamiliar world.

It is in this moment of losing our connection to our Big Soul that the fear-based *I* of our Little Soul is born. *I am separate, I am alone, I don't know where I am, I don't know how to be.* Later in this chapter, we'll explore *why* and *how* our Little Soul loses its connection to Big Soul. For now, let's just explore the result of that break.

As your lost and disconnected Little Soul starts looking for its true source of comfort, Big Soul, it comes across other sources that inadequately mimic how it feels to be in Big Soul's presence. What it finds instead is a bewildering number of rules about how it is supposed to behave and who it is supposed to be to receive that comfort.

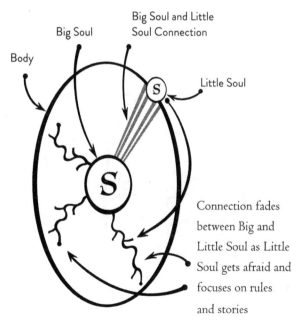

Big Soul and Little
Soul Connection

Big Soul

Body

Little Soul

Connection fades
between Big and
Little Soul as Little
Soul gets afraid and
focuses on rules
and stories

Without your Big Soul's big-picture guidance, your Little Soul starts soaking up new concepts and beliefs that are not highest truth but only appear to be truth. Little Soul is then introduced to the concept of punishment and reward and begins to fear the pain of love being withheld. As a result, Little Soul concludes that it is not enough and believes that the only safety is in fitting in, or that the only safety is to rebel and not fit in. In either case, your Little Soul grasps for an identity to give it a sense of stability in a very confusing world.

Your Little Soul spends years carefully constructing who it believes it is supposed to be to be loved and accepted. Each time it believes a thought about how it is supposed to be, such as *I should be happy all the time,* or *If I'm happy, people will be jealous of me,* or *If I were good enough, I'd make lots of money,* or *My friends won't approve of me if I let them know I love baseball,* your Little Soul erects

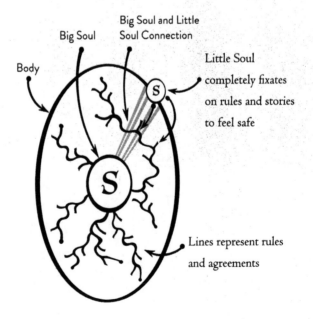

Big Soul and Little
Soul Connection

Big Soul

Body

Little Soul
completely fixates
on rules and stories
to feel safe

Lines represent rules
and agreements

tiny walls that further separate it from its connection to its own Big Soul truth.

Remember, Big Soul hasn't gone anywhere. Rather, your Little Soul *believes* it is lost and alone and can't find its way back to its source. There are always glimmers of Big Soul peeking through, showing the way home. But your Little Soul is so distracted by thinking about how to be that these glimpses of simply being are quickly covered over by stories.

## The Little Soul's Fear

Here is a specific look at how our Little Soul loses its way, taken from my book *A Little Book on Big Freedom*:

I am three years old, playing with my rambunctious eight-year-old sister. We're laughing and gleefully running around the house, arms waving, feet barely touching the ground.

Suddenly, I hear a loud noise behind me, and I turn to see that my sister has accidentally knocked over a vase, which has shattered all over the floor. We freeze and look at each other, wondering what to do next. My sister shakes her head and says, "We'd better clean this up before Mom comes back inside." But when we go into the kitchen to get the broom, we decide to have a snack first. Before long, the two of us are laughing and playing again, forgetting all about the vase.

Meanwhile, our mom has been outside working in the garden. She is hot, tired, and still upset over an argument she had with Dad earlier in the day. She's thinking about everything she needs to get done, and trying to fortify herself to push through her current state of physical and emotional overwhelm.

Mom's not-good day is about to get worse.

As she walks into the house, she hears my sister and me laughing and running around. Then she sees her grandmother's vase—*the only thing her grandmother had ever given her*—shattered on the floor.

Even though she has rarely yelled or gotten upset with us, today she just loses it. She starts yelling, "Who broke my vase?! Who broke my vase?!"

My sister and I come running into the front room, both scared as she shouts at us about the vase, demanding to know who broke it.

In a panic, my sister points at me and says, "She did it!"

I look at her, and then at my mother, stuttering, "I . . . I . . . I didn't—"

"You! Go to your room now!" Mom yells.

Now close your eyes for a moment and imagine that you are a child and that you have just been punished for something you didn't do. How does this feel in your body? What thoughts are beginning to cycle through your mind?

You may have a strong emotional reaction, a tingling that fills you from head to toe. Physically, you may feel a churning in your stomach, a tightness in your throat, or a tearing feeling in your chest. You may be angry and feel betrayed. You may feel scared or confused.

The emotion itself is not the problem, but *what we do next* creates the fodder for most of our ongoing suffering as adults.

We tell ourselves a story.

As a little kid, consider some of the things you may tell your-self to help make sense of what just happened:

*Mom loves my sister more than she loves me.*
*People will lie or betray me to serve their own interest.*
*If I lie, I won't get punished.*
*It's not safe to play or feel joy; I'll get in trouble.*
*I can't trust Mom.*
*I have to be extra careful and earn the feeling of love and safety.*
*I'm bad, clumsy, and stupid.*
*Material objects are more important than people.*
*Life's not fair.*

Any one of these thoughts could be nothing—like a dande-lion puff blowing in the wind and not taking root. Or the puff could land on fertile soil and start growing roots and shoot-ing out leaves. Before you know it, a whole field of weeds has sprouted. These tiny thoughts have immense power—not their own power but the power we give to them. We are incredible creators, but what we often create is based on the seeds of false thoughts that, when planted, take root and blossom into *agree-ments* that we make with ourselves and with others.

While the situation with the vase is a relatively minor trauma, the point is to see how a brief incident can plant seeds of doubt, confusion, and misunderstanding, which can then grow into larger agreements that affect our entire lives until we investigate and uproot them. The child in this scenario may not even remember the incident when she grows up, but you can see the impact it could have on her thinking—especially if things like this occur on a regular basis. On an unconscious level, she will literally create a reality that will grow from this handful of childhood agreements. These beliefs will become a shaky floor for all her future actions.

Take a moment to reflect on your own experiences:

Where have you erected jail-like walls based on past stories?

What are the stories you tell yourself that make you feel helpless or victimized instead of powerful and confident?

In what ways do they limit how you perceive your life story, your talents, and your possibilities for the future?

For many of us, there are more than a few of these in a variety of areas. Sometimes we have told ourselves these stories for so long that we no longer recognize them as stories. We mistake them for "the way things are." Unearthing these beliefs can take time and energy, but we must reveal and expunge them if we are going to be free.

The good news is that you do not need to know the origin of these beliefs to correct and replace them; all you need to do is (1) be honest with yourself about the current state of your internal house; and (2) be willing to do the work to remodel it from the ground up.

We are incredible creators, but what we often create is based on a foundation of false thoughts from which we then build an entire, limiting structure of agreements. As don Miguel writes in *The Four Agreements Companion Book*, "Imagine every agreement is like a brick. Humans create an entire structure out of bricks, and we glue it together with our faith. We believe without doubt in all the knowledge within the structure. Our faith gets trapped inside that structure because we put our faith in each agreement. It's not important if it is or isn't true; we believe it, and for us it is true."

Let's continue to explore how a thought forms the basis of a story that hardens into a structure that walls us off from the wisdom of our Big Soul. Imagine yourself as the little kid who got punished for breaking the vase. Let's pretend that you have the thought, *I got punished because Mom loves my sister more than she loves me.* While it might feel awful to think this thought, do you notice that there is also a sense of relief at having a reason for being punished, even if it is not true?

Now imagine that your mom comes into your room and apologizes for yelling at you. She says all the "right" things: "I'm so sorry, honey. I had a rotten day and I loved that vase, so I got upset. Your sister just told me she knocked the vase over by accident and that it wasn't your fault. I love you, and I'm sorry I yelled at you and sent you to your room. Come, let's go have dinner."

But what little doubt has already been planted in your mind? As you sit down to dinner, imagine Mom passes the mashed potatoes to your sibling first. If you are still holding the thought *Mom loves my sister more,* what would you say to yourself?

Your oh-so-helpful brain would do what we call *selective-evidence gathering.* You might think, *Aha! I knew it! Mom passed the mashed potatoes to her first. She does love her more.* And later, if Mom passes you the ice cream first, what might you do with that evidence? Often when you have a seed thought, you will begin to gather evidence to make sense of the thought. If there is an experience that does not support the story, you actually ignore it, or you weave it into your new story. In this way, you are ingenious! So you might think, *Yeah, Mom passed me the ice cream first, but it is just because she is feeling guilty that she loves my sister more than she loves me.*

Do you see how you can take one thought and build a whole elaborate structure, a fortress created by ideas and conditions and agreements about what is true and what is not?

*Mom likes my sister better, but I don't care anyway. I don't need anyone. Mom likes my sister better because I am bad. Mom likes my sister better because younger sisters are more important. Maybe if I am perfect, if I try really hard, then I'll be loved like my sister is. Or maybe if I am invisible, if no one sees me and I am really quiet and nice, I won't get in trouble.* The foundational bricks of this new internal structure—*I am bad, I don't need anyone,* and *Younger sisters are more important*—will produce more and more agreements that become bricks as long as she is not conscious of them. She will create a walled-in reality that will conform to this handful of unconscious childhood agreements, all so that she can feel safe.

How have you created your current reality based on old stories or agreements you made with yourself, about what you were told as a child? And why are these false stories so alluring that you could forget the warmth of your Big Soul? Let's take a look.

As children, each of us took on beliefs or agreements that moved us further away from our Big Soul. Many of these agreements, which are designed to give us a sense of safety when we feel lost and confused, were passed on energetically from our parents and other caretakers. Some we mimicked from what we saw around us, and others we made up all on our own, like believing *Mom loves my sister more* in the scenario illustrated above. However, the stories we created as a child were highly influenced not only by the agreements of the people around us but also by what the Toltecs call *the dream of the planet*—humanity's collective perspective. As don Miguel and his son don Jose describe in *The Fifth Agreement:* "The shared dream of humanity, the dream of the planet, was there before you were born, and this is how you learned to create your own art, the story of you."

You can easily see the invisible but pervasive influence of the dream of the planet by turning on the nightly news, reading the headlines of major newspapers, watching soap operas, or looking at advertisements. When was the last time you saw a major evening news story that highlighted all the good things happening in the world? Or how about a soap opera where the characters didn't end up knee deep in painful emotional drama? Or saw an advertisement about how perfect you are and would you care to buy this new shampoo? Most media report fear and scarcity; advertising is geared to how perfect you would be if you used their product, not how perfect you are now. . . .

The information on how to think and how to act and how to be is not created by the media—it is merely a reflection of the agreements we've made. The content of our media shows us that most of us are experiencing reality through the eyes of conflict, fear, scarcity, and a sense of not being good enough. These limiting qualities are what hook our attention because they feel familiar to us, and in that familiarity, we find a (false) sense of safety.

Since almost everyone—from our parents to our teachers to our friends—is immersed in this way of perceiving the world, it seems natural for us to believe that we are not lovable or that we have to be a certain way to be accepted. But this is not our natural state, and that's why it feels so uncomfortable to us! That's why we are always looking for comfort and for something to complete us. That's why we are seeking the path home.

## Finding Our Way Back Home

Your Big Soul is like the sun, constantly radiating its loving glow. No matter how lost you feel, how much you are suffering, or how deeply ingrained your stories or agreements are, at any moment, your Little Soul can *choose* to pierce through the illusion of separateness to return home to the ancient and wise guidance of your Big Soul. This takes a willingness (and a constantly honed skill) to release the stories of the past and turn toward the truth of this present moment. It is in the present that we can cut through the illusion of our old, fear-based agreements and reconnect our Little Soul with the calm, peaceful, and steady love of our Big Soul.

The love and comfort your Little Soul seeks will not be filled by the temporary pleasures of life. No matter how good the wine, how abundant the chocolate, or how many likes and comments you have on Facebook, when your Little Soul is disconnected from your Big Soul, all relief is transitory. But even in your darkest times, your Big Soul holds up a lantern, waiting patiently for your wandering Little Soul to come home. The path back to Big Soul is there but is simply obscured by the walls you have built.

Keep stepping out of your Little Soul's perspective and hold the big-picture view. You are not your Little Soul. You are not the fear-based structures that lie between your Little Soul and Big Soul. And you are not just your Big Soul. You are Little Soul and Big Soul, both yearning to be reunited.

When you learn to witness the totality of your physical/ mental/emotional being through the eyes of Big Soul rather than through the eyes of Little Soul, everything changes. With this one perceptual shift, you can go from feeling stuck to being full of ease, from a place of judgment to one of compassion, from a state of annoyance to one of acceptance. But learning to stabilize Big Soul perspective can take a lifetime. This is why we need tools like the Warrior Heart practice to help us break down the walls, at first brick by brick, and then wall by wall, ultimately allowing our Little Soul to be freed from its self-imposed jail so that it can see new possibilities and perspectives.

Your Big Soul doesn't impatiently demand that your Little Soul be different. Your Big Soul isn't addicted to caretaking or fixing the Little Soul. It knows that the Little Soul will eventually figure its way through the fog and break down the false walls. Remember, Big Soul is like an ancient grandma who patiently and sweetly invites you to remember that you are so much more than your beliefs and fears.

Your Big Soul eternally whispers to your Little Soul, "You are enough exactly the way you are. You are all of creation. You are loved. You are perfect the way you are." Your Big Soul is always holding out a hand and saying, "Let's explore and create in this wonderful world of taste, touch, sight, sound, and feeling!"

While your Big Soul constantly sends your Little Soul, your little lost ego-personality, love notes and trails of bread crumbs leading the way home, it can be hard to see the path. The quiet, steady voice of your Big Soul can easily be drowned out by the noise of your stories. The moments of grace, the peaceful pauses, and the exhilarating insights are often quickly swamped with unsupportive thoughts and emotional reactions.

This is why you can have awareness of a pattern or habit you want to transform, but find it nearly impossible to change your behavior. If you have ever wanted to stop thinking about an ex, or refrain from being upset by your boss's curtness, or have faith but instead find yourself anxious and worried about your future, you know how fixated and freaked out your Little Soul can be.

Having a desire of what you want in your life is only a start. It is not enough to simply understand that you should not judge yourself or to understand intellectually that you are safe even when someone is angry at you. The question is, how do you fully embody your choice and presence in each moment rather than just thinking about it or wishing for it?

This is the path of the Warrior Heart, which will help connect the stormy waters of your fear-based thoughts and emotions to reconnect your Big Soul and your Little Soul. Instead of fighting your Little Soul or trying to force the waters of your mind and emotions to be calm, let's build a bridge. Just as it took time to build the old structures of fear and separation, it will take action and focus to lay a new pathway between your Big Soul and ego-personality.

Your Warrior Heart awakens the moment you start loving the journey of reconnecting your Little Soul to your Big Soul's loving guidance and grace. It is about accepting all of you, big and little, whether your experience is blissful expansion or painful contraction. Being a Warrior of the Heart brings you back into alignment with the beauty of all of you, including your Little Soul ego-personality. It is this acceptance that clears the smoke and bridges the gap between your Big Soul and your Little Soul. And once this happens, everything changes as you realign with your true, wise inner self.

There are two main actions that reconnect your Big Soul and your Little Soul. The first is to do more of what you love. (Isn't that a great assignment?) Doing more of what you love can actually be more difficult to do than it seems. Here's why.

When you do something you love (like hiking or dancing or daydreaming or running or knitting or whatever floats your boat!), you get completely and happily lost in the activity. Your mind quiets, and in that space, your Little Soul and Big Soul are united again, able to work together creatively toward solutions or simply enjoy being. You don't have any need to explain, defend, judge, or worry. All is right in the world, because your Little Soul is in the present moment, holding hands with your Big Soul.

Losing yourself through doing things you love is very different from using an activity to numb or distract yourself (like compulsive drinking or shopping). The same action can reconnect your Little Soul with your Big Soul or create even more separation, depending on the intention you are bringing to it. While substances that alter your consciousness can be useful for getting past the mind and merging with your Big Soul, they are best used as a flashlight that points you in the direction you want to go so that you can then find your way there on your own, rather than use it as a crutch that will ultimately cause more harm.

So your first task is to do more of what you love so you touch the happy-wise place within you.

Your second task is cleaning out everything that is between Little Soul and your Big Soul. This means facing and dissolving all the agreements, fears, false beliefs, past trauma, hurts, and stuck places.

Now, cleaning is not usually considered a very glamorous or enticing spiritual or healing endeavor. We would much rather have things disappear or change on their own or have someone to come in and clean things up for us. Or sometimes we hope that if we just go to enough workshops or see the right healer or meditate just the right way, we can somehow skip straight to blissful enlightenment (or at least be free of our mind's insanity).

In the Toltec teachings, there are three main levels of mastery: awareness, transformation, and intent. In the first level, you learn to become aware of your thoughts, emotions, and body, without judgment or victimization. As your awareness grows, you see and take action on what agreements and habits you want to transform. Instead of being stuck repeating the same patterns and responding with the same emotional reactions, you begin to consciously transform how you behave and think. As you change your thinking and behaviors, you align more and more with your Big Soul's wisdom instead of your Little Soul's fear. And eventually, you step into living from intent, which means living in inspiration, faith, and connection to your Big Soul.

My philosophy is this: May we become immersed in doing things we love, or use everything in our lives to help us clean up what blocks us from loving the moment we are in. There are plenty of challenges in our lives, and avoiding or ignoring the challenges is not the pathway to freedom. Your freedom comes from learning to courageously face your challenges as opportunities to clean out false beliefs and old, heavy emotions.

And for this, you need a Warrior Heart.

## Practice

Before we move to exploring the four chambers of the Warrior Heart practice, take a few moments to write in a journal to help you uncover the Little Soul stories you tell yourself. Use these questions to guide you. Write without thinking, and see what you learn about both your foundational agreements and the walls that your Little Soul has created to feel safe.

What sort of experiences do you find happening in your life over and over again?

What beliefs or agreements did you learn from your parents?

How do you feel about yourself?

How do you feel about the world?

What things do you judge about yourself the most?

How do you judge others?

What beliefs or agreements are limiting you?

# 2

# Introducing the Chambers

*Three things cannot be long hidden: the sun,*
*the moon, and the truth.*

—BUDDHA

THE NUMBER ONE QUESTION I am asked is "How do I clean out all the agreements, stories, and experiences that don't serve me?" And the answer is the foundational practice that is laid out in this book.

The Warrior Heart practice is one of the most efficient, practical, and doable methods of inner cleaning you'll find. As you incorporate the Warrior Heart practice into your life, you'll find that you no longer wonder why you are upset, or get stuck in painful thoughts and emotions. You'll learn how to stop taking things personally, be able to release the weight of your past traumas and experiences, and quickly clear out old beliefs and reactions that no longer serve you so you can get to the truth.

Now let me introduce you to the four chambers that comprise the power-washing brilliance of the Warrior Heart practice and will help you step into your own warrior self.

## *The Four Chambers*

Feeling
Story
Truth
Intent

These are the four chambers of the Warrior Heart practice. Learning how to work with the chambers will change the way you operate in the world by helping you release limiting and painful beliefs and to rearrange the pieces of your personal puzzles into an integrated new whole—mentally, emotionally, and physically.

The idea of personal transformation is just an idea until you fully commit to taking action. But it is also important to know *how* to take action.

The Warrior Heart practice centers around four distinct chambers, which are like the four vital chambers of the heart. It takes both the courage of a warrior and the vulnerability of an open heart to step into each of these "rooms" and witness all of yourself, including and primarily your emotions, thoughts, truth, and wisdom.

Just like the heart, no one chamber is more important than the others; they all work together. There's a continual flow that happens in our heart as we work through the chambers. In the following chapters, we will go through each chamber sequentially, but please consider this model as circular rather than linear.

The four chambers of the Warrior Heart practice are:

## THE FEELING CHAMBER

You enter the Warrior Heart practice by learning to gently sit with emotional triggers, fears, or pain that arises within you, *separate from the story* you believe is causing the emotion. In the Feeling Chamber, you learn how to be present with discomfort and become curious about what is actually happening in your physical and emotional body rather than just thinking about the upset, trying to repress emotions, or cycling stories endlessly. In the Feeling Chamber, the goal is not to fix, understand, or explain emotions but to simply be with them consciously.

### The Questions You Bring to the Feeling Chamber Are:

- What am I feeling?
- How does it affect my physical body?
- Where do I feel closed and where do I feel open?
- How can I support myself to stay open to my discomfort?

The keys to unlocking the Feeling Chamber are breath and presence.

## THE STORY CHAMBER

Once you have spent some time breathing, witnessing, and feeling your emotions and how they affect your physical body, you will move to the Story Chamber. Here you give yourself full permission to let your judgments, fears, worst-case scenarios, doubts, and insecurities speak without censorship. You invite those parts of you that feel victimized by your inner critic, other people, and the world to share their story. You follow the threads of old story lines deeper into where hurtful words, hatred, and longing are hiding. You learn to stay curious, witnessing each story as it unfolds from past and present as well as those story themes that try to fix or explain or threaten to haunt your future.

## The Questions You Bring to the Story Chamber Are:

- What am I telling myself?
- What words have I woven together?
- What old agreements and rules are embedded in my story?
- How can I support myself in listening to a deeper layer of this story?

The keys to opening the Story Chamber are willingness and permission.

### THE TRUTH CHAMBER

While the Story Chamber gives you information on the multifaceted and noisy layers of your internal dialogue, the Truth Chamber opens up space for stillness. You cross a threshold between Story and Truth, where you must leave behind being right, being wrong, being understood, or any other desire. You move toward the simplicity of what is real in this moment. Most people enter the Truth Chamber dragging their story with them like a familiar blanket they can't let go of, and they believe that creating a better, more spiritual, or more pleasing story is the truth. In the Truth Chamber, you explore the difference between ultimate truth and subjective truth.

I always like to start with the basics in the Truth Chamber: I am breathing. Truth. I am here. Truth. Using these two truths allows you to begin to build a foundation for carefully exploring and separating out the threads of your story from truth.

**The Questions You Bring to the Truth Chamber Are:**

- What is an ultimate truth right now?
- What is true about this situation?
- What do I wish were true versus what is actually a fact?
- How can I support myself in being with the truth?

The keys to opening the door of the Truth Chamber are creating a sense of spaciousness inside and the ability to listen to what is true.

### THE INTENT CHAMBER

The Truth Chamber opens up space so that you can step into the Intent Chamber and get clear about what you really want in each situation. Your intent is your focus and 100 percent commitment. Without intent, you are at the mercy of outside forces, even when you are clear about the truth. Having clarity about your truth is like patching the holes in your sails after they have been torn in the storm of a story; your intent is your steady hand on the ropes, allowing you to catch the wind and consciously navigate where you want to go.

Your intent is critical because it guides your coming actions. The choices you make going forward may be different if your intent is "compassion" versus "speaking my truth no matter what."

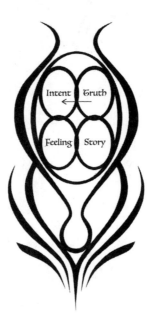

### The Questions You Bring to the Intent Chamber Are:

- What do I actually want in this situation?
- Where do I want to put my focus?

- What is my bigger focus in life right now, and how does this situation fit in?
- What word best describes where I want to put my attention?

The keys to opening the Intent Chamber are in taking total responsibility for your life and your choices and claiming your personal accountability and direction.

## *Circling Back*

The Warrior Heart practice does not end here. The real potency of the Warrior Heart practice is what happens next: You go back through the chambers. Once you are clear on your Intent, you step back into the Truth Chamber. I like to imagine that you revisit the Truth with new eyes, holding your Intent in one hand and your Truth in the other as you step back into the Story Chamber, where the view is now very different.

The process of moving from Story to Truth to Intent and back again will help you to integrate a more expansive view of those places where you were once struggling. In your second visit to the Story Chamber, you will review and rewrite your story to align with the truth rather than your fears and old beliefs. You will be freed from what you think should be happening and be released from weighty expectations and subconscious obligations. This will allow you to be creative and playful in your relationship with your story. Even if the story itself remains a difficult one, your relationship to the story changes from victimization or judgment to power and curiosity.

The final step in the Warrior Heart practice is to return to the beginning, the Feeling Chamber.

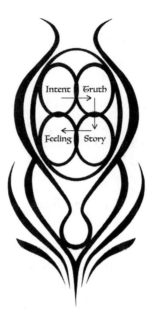

The Warrior Heart practice is like a sponge that is always available for you to clean up your internal and external messes, which then allows you to return to clarity, peace, and authentic communication.

As you use the Warrior Heart practice to consciously reconnect your Little Soul and your Big Soul as allies, you will return to your natural state: whole and joyful. Always remember that you are Big Soul, vitally connected and complete, *and* you are also that fearful child who needs to be reconnected and reminded of the truth. With this awareness of what is truth and what is not, you can clean up the Little Soul's mistaken perceptions and false stories. And the more you clean away the debris, the more your Big Soul can shine through your Little Soul and out into the world.

You can use the Warrior Heart practice to understand more about an emotion or reaction you are having, how to determine the best course of action, clean old agreements, get more information on something you are blocked about, move past fears or procrastination, and be able to do this as a daily practice. It is a versatile tool, and as you use it, you will come up with more ways that it can help you find clarity, peace, and direction.

Over the next four chapters, we will dive into learning about the individual chambers and how to navigate them. Then I'll introduce you to an advanced daily practice called *stalking* that will help you integrate the Warrior Heart practice even more effectively.

Throughout each of the descriptions of the chambers, I will share my own experiences and bring in specific, real-life stories to help you in your process. We will talk about how people have used the Warrior Heart practice to untangle specific challenges, similar to your own. We will explore the Warrior Heart practice using tangible topics, such as caring for elderly parents, divorce, troubled children, aging, health issues, work challenges, finances, and more.

Throughout the coming chapters, we will also explore Toltec concepts of the first, second, and third attention, the concepts of the *nagual* and the *tonal*, the *petty tyrant, not doings*, and more (see glossary for definitions). These ancient teachings are brought forward with a gentle, feminine touch that will allow you to incorporate them with ease rather than through forceful, "cut off from your emotions and change your life now" emphasis that can sometimes haunt other Toltec and inquiry-based practices.

As we step into the chambers, take a moment to close your eyes and pick one issue or struggle that you keep getting snagged by.

**Reflect on the issue that you keep coming back to over and**

**over in your mind, even if you know it is not true.** The issue might be around relationships, finances, your spiritual path, your health. . . . What's one area that keeps snagging you? Write it down as concisely as possible and do your best not to judge yourself or try to fix it. Then as you learn more about each of the chambers, I'll teach you how to use the Warrior Heart practice to clean your old story.

You can download a free Warrior Heart practice sheet at www.heatherashamara.com/whp-sheet. This will give you a format to write out the information you gather from the practice. As you go through the chapters in *The Warrior Heart Practice,* I support you in keeping a few Warrior Heart practice sheets available so that if something arises, you can write it down while it's fresh in your mind, and capture your process. You can also create a Warrior Heart practice binder, where you keep all of your practice sheets so you can look back and see your progress. Look for many more helpful suggestions in the Exercises section after each chapter.

And now, on to becoming more intimate with the four chambers of the Warrior Heart practice.

# 3

# The Feeling Chamber

*Courage has roots. She sleeps on a futon on the floor and lives
close to the ground. Courage looks you straight in the eye. She
is not impressed with powertrippers and she knows first aid.
Courage is not afraid to weep and she is not afraid to pray,
even when she is not sure who she is praying to. When Courage
walks, it is clear that she has made the journey from loneliness
to solitude. The people who told me she is stern were not lying,
they just forgot to mention that she is kind.*

—J. RUTH GENDLER, *THE BOOK OF QUALITIES*

THE FIRST TIME I actually decided to go toward rather
than run away from a difficult emotion, it was a revelation.
And a total life-changer.

When I was fourteen years old, I remember making a decision about emotions, which, for many years, affected me in a
negative way.

My parents had just told my sister and me that we were moving from Bangkok, Thailand, where we had lived for the past
two wonderful years, to the tiny island of Singapore.

I remember going numb at the time. I think I was in shock.

I'd finally settled into my life overseas after leaving my gang of California friends. I couldn't comprehend that we were moving again. I remember calling my "boyfriend" (we had kissed once), and before he picked up the phone, I had already decided I was not going to feel anything.

So, in a robotic manner, I told him I was moving and hung up the phone. And then, true to my word, I didn't let myself feel. No grief, no upset, no problem. But of course, it was a big problem.

In Singapore, I did make new friends, fell in love with my first real boyfriend, and excelled in the sports I had chosen—track and competitive horseback riding. But a part of me remained hollow. The unexpressed grief that I never let myself experience kept me feeling empty and disconnected.

So I spent much of my early twenties avoiding my emotions. I drank too much. I fixated on my boyfriend. I worried about things I had no control over to avoid emotions that I felt would drown me.

When I went to college and became very involved in social justice and activism, that old grief came out as rage. It didn't stop the hollow feeling; however, it did make me feel more powerful and justified in my anger. "This is not fair, and I will fix it!!!" became my rallying cry in regard to apartheid, sexual abuse, the environment, and civil rights for gays, blacks, and other minorities. I was dedicated but not truly effective because I was hiding from myself.

And then, late one night while in a coffee plantation in Nicaragua, my grief surfaced all at once. It was triggered by the poverty and war that I was witnessing all around me. I realized that no matter how many medical supplies or toys or vehicles I helped bring to alleviate the suffering (I had been part of a caravan that drove for ten days from California through Mexico,

Guatemala, and Honduras into Nicaragua), it was not really going to solve anything. I felt helpless. And for some unknown reason, I stopped avoiding my emotions and let myself feel.

The tears flowed and just wouldn't stop. I cried for the children that were being killed. I cried for the people who lived on the coffee plantation where we worked, because they had no running water and no resources. I cried for the American aid worker who had recently been killed.

And then I realized I was really crying for myself.

All the hurt and sadness and despair of my fourteen-year-old self flooded in. And I let it. On that dirt floor in the jungle, I let the tears and snot and sorrow melt the armor I had built around my heart. And the next day, I woke up feeling softer, more present, and filled with compassion for myself and the numerous challenges of being human. I knew that all I could really bring was my love, compassion, and care. And so, as I picked coffee beans the next day, I made eye contact with the others in the field. I smiled. I let people know I saw them, I was there, and I was respectful of their strength and perseverance.

It took me a long time to integrate the realization that letting the emotions move through me brought relief, gratitude, and insight.

Now—many years later and after a lot of dedicated therapy, spiritual work, and emotional cleaning—I can say one thing is true.

Being a Warrior of the Heart takes great courage.

Unlike the courage it takes to bungee jump or skydive, it takes even greater courage to face yourself—specifically, the courage to turn toward your emotions.

This is where we start the practice in the *Feeling Chamber*, courageously learning how to authentically experience our emotions.

Why start with our emotional body?

As humans, we have a strong tendency to live in our mind and tell ourselves stories as a way to avoid the emotions that are actually going on within us. Often when we sense an uncomfortable situation or emotion, we immediately distract ourselves or pop up into our head. Instead of being curious about our emotions ("Hey, I wonder what is going on within me and what I am really feeling?"), we analyze, criticize, or demonize the emotions to avoid actually feeling them. Our inner safety mechanism leads us to exit our emotional body in all sorts of creative ways. We will talk more about these exits later on in the book.

You may also see yourself or others doing the opposite of emotional avoidance. We can become swamped by them. I call this *getting stuck in the spin cycle*. Being caught in a spin cycle happens when your emotions and your story get tangled together in such a way that the story is constantly triggering the emotion. This is similar to when a nerve gets pinched and causes excruciating pain every time you move. Learning the Warrior Heart practice will help you separate the Feeling from the Story and free you from chronic emotional pain.

The result of either avoiding or cycling your emotions is monumental. Avoiding your emotions leads to addiction, anxiety, stress, and disease. On the other hand, when you get stuck experiencing an old emotion over and over again—frustration, jealousy, rage, a sense of betrayal, worry—you are not clearing it; you are only exhausting yourself, running down your adrenal system, and creating inner and outer drama. It is like getting stuck in first gear and being forced to drive down the same road over and over again. The scenery never changes, and you are definitely not living to your fullest expression.

Doctors are now saying that up to 80 percent of today's

ailments are not created by stress as previously thought but by emotional repression or cycling. Unprocessed grief, anger, fear, guilt, and shame are literally making us sick. Stagnant emotions or emotions that we cycle (experiencing over and over again in a draining way) weigh us down with toxic thoughts and sluggish energy.

But there is a way through.

## Moving Toward the Discomfort

In my book *Awaken Your Inner Fire*, I share a very helpful metaphor regarding the emotional body:

> Imagine wearing a big backpack filled with all of the unexpressed emotions you've collected over the course of your life. Some of these you may have consciously put in the backpack, like when you have said to yourself, "I don't want to feel this," and you pushed something down. Others were unconsciously added, perhaps because you didn't understand what you were feeling at the time or you simply didn't know how to effectively express the emotion. Some of these emotions come from way back, and without realizing it you have been carrying them around for many years—like when your father walked out of your life when you were seven, or your refusal to shed tears after a classmate said you were ugly when you were a child, or even the immense love you felt for your high school classmate that you shut down because it was unrequited.
>
> These emotions haven't gone away even though you may not think about them regularly. What I've found is

that they can be reactivated in our daily life when new situations trigger them, even though we often aren't conscious of the connection.

So instead of ignoring the weight of that old emotion-filled backpack, or trying to get someone else to take responsibility for what is in it (*You are making me feel this way!*), let's make the agreement to set the backpack down and peer inside. This is a radical act of actually unpacking your emotions as a curious witness, rather than viewing them as a constant enemy to ignore or gossip about.

Opening up to your emotions means you are willing to turn and face your anxiety, fear, and upset instead of exiting the discomfort through distraction, addiction, or projection. Like all of us, you probably have many creative ways to exit so that you don't feel your emotions. By naming your exits, you can teach yourself to get steady and enter into the Feeling Chamber.

Here is one of my favorite poems, "The Guest House," from the great Sufi mystic Jalal ad-Din Rumi, which gently speaks to what I am saying:

> *This being human is a guest house.*
> *Every morning a new arrival.*
>
> *A joy, a depression, a meanness,*
> *some momentary awareness comes*
> *as an unexpected visitor.*
>
> *Welcome and entertain them all!*
> *Even if they're a crowd of sorrows,*
> *who violently sweep your house*
> *empty of its furniture,*

*still treat each guest honorably.*
*He may be clearing you out*
*for some new delight.*

*The dark thought, the shame, the malice,*
*meet them at the door laughing,*
*and invite them in.*
*Be grateful for whoever comes,*
*because each has been sent*
*as a guide from beyond.*

Written in the thirteenth century, Rumi's words speak to the vital importance that we treat our emotional body with respect, knowing that our emotions are guides to help us bring more intimacy, delight, and gratitude into every moment.

What do you do when old emotions come knocking at your door wanting to be let in?

Do you usually get busy, distract yourself, blame someone else, or go numb?

The process of learning to open the door, as Rumi says in "The Guest House," is to trade in fear, denial, or avoidance for curiosity, patience, and more curiosity.

## Maria: Learning to Be with Emotions

My family always avoided emotions; we never talked about anything. I remember being really confused as a young adult because I would feel things so deeply but knew I couldn't express what was going on.

When I first started doing the Warrior Heart practice, I had no idea how to sit with my emotions. It felt completely foreign and even dangerous. I started small each day, just asking myself, *What are you feeling now?* For a while, I didn't think it was working. And then one day, I had a huge emotional reaction to something my boyfriend said on the phone. I started to squash it, to pretend everything was all right, but it wouldn't go away. I got off the phone as quickly as I could and asked myself, *Okay, what are you feeling?*

And, *bam,* it was like a waterfall hit. I started crying and realized I was feeling jealous. (My boyfriend was visiting family, and his first girlfriend was coming over for lunch.) I stayed with the feeling and practiced breathing and being with the sensations. And as I breathed into my belly and just felt the jealousy, I realized it was not going to kill me. I could feel the feeling and survive. It was a total gift, and it allowed me to later talk to my boyfriend about my fears in a healthy, nonreactive way. Now I welcome my emotions and am always curious what they are helping me learn about myself.

To learn how to be with your emotions and sit in the Feeling Chamber, you must first be honest about where you usually exit to avoid your emotions.

Okay, Warrior Heart, it's time to name your exits and learn to hold yourself in love as you step toward healing your old emotional wounding and fears. I'm here with you; we can do this together. Let's trade fear for courage and armor for freedom.

## *Naming Your Exits*

In their book, *Undefended Love*, authors Jett Psaris and Marlena Lyons list ways that we exit when our emotions become too uncomfortable during an argument with another person. (One of my personal favorites is frantic housecleaning.) Everything in this list can translate into ways we exit our own emotions.

Here are some of their examples of exits:

**Leave physically:** walk out, get sick, have accidents, feel paralyzed, clean the house, exercise, fall asleep

**Leave emotionally:** become confused, shut down, get angry, talk incessantly, go silent, experience self-doubt, become ambivalent

**Leave mentally:** agree to forget about the fight, change the subject, make mental lists, intellectualize, analyze, rationalize, go blank, count

**Defend:** lie, get indignant, become self-righteous, justify, feel criticized, resent

**Indulge in addiction:** shop, eat, watch television, use drugs and alcohol, act out sexually, relate compulsively, work, engage in fantasy, gamble

When we leave physically, emotionally, or mentally, we are removing ourselves from the Feeling Chamber and actually from our lives. Even the simplest things, like exercising or email, can become a way to avoid the discomfort of sitting with our emotions. This doesn't mean that every time you clean the house or exercise, you are dodging your emotions, but it is worth watching yourself to see what actions you take to exit your emotional body.

Sometimes we emotionally exit by becoming confused or trading one emotion for another. Confusion is a sure sign that there is an emotion that needs our attention. And be aware of the times when you go to habitual anger or frustration when in fact there is another emotion you are avoiding.

Most of us are highly skilled at intellectualizing and rationalizing our emotions instead of feeling them. We think about why we are sad or justify our anger and end up being in a kind of limbo where we can't actually clear the emotion.

I've also witnessed people who are on a spiritual or healing path sometimes use "being spiritual" as a way to avoid their messy, distasteful, "nonspiritual" emotions. In fantasy, spiritual people do not have anger or jealousy or sadness. The unspoken belief is that we should be able to avoid the uncomfortable parts of being human through meditation or using the right crystals or the right mantra. The result is a lingering sense of being "bad" or a feeling of flatness when we sever the tie between ourselves and our emotions.

One woman I taught the Warrior Heart practice to was shocked to realize, "I have spent the last fifteen years using my spiritual practice to avoid my emotions!" Unfortunately, this is not an uncommon realization. Spiritual practice is not designed to help you avoid all suffering but to learn to sit with your emotions with love and transform them through your presence and conscious untangling of emotions and story.

## Will: Holding Myself Through
## My Father's Illness

My father started having dizzy spells and losing his balance about two years ago. Every time I would hear about one of his episodes, I would immediately change the subject and start talking about something else. I couldn't handle the emotions associated with his aging and knowing that I was going to lose him one day. (My mother died when I was two years old.) As his illness progressed (he was eventually diagnosed with a rare form of cancer), I not only started avoiding conversations with my brother, who lived close to my dad, I also started drinking more and more wine to cope with my fears.

I didn't connect how I was using avoidance and alcohol to exit my emotions until I started doing the Warrior Heart practice. The first question, "What are you feeling?" was so uncomfortable. I didn't want to feel. But I also knew I couldn't continue on as I was. My drinking was starting to affect my work and my relationships, especially with my children.

When I first imagined myself sitting in the Feeling Chamber, I panicked and immediately had a glass of wine and watched a movie to distance myself from the intensity of my emotions. But I stayed with it, every day asking myself, *What are you feeling?* until I had a breakthrough. Finally, I let myself feel my own terror at the thought of losing my father. What surprised me was that once I let myself feel it, I realized that if I didn't face the fear, I was going to miss the rest of my father's life and I would regret that terribly. As I turned and faced the fear, I made the commitment to

myself to learn to be strong for my father, myself, and especially my kids. I started going to twelve-step meetings and
found a friend who worked in hospice that helped me understand how I could best support my father, and myself, during this time. I started traveling to visit with him, often just
sitting and holding his hand. Instead of avoiding the feelings,
I started sharing about what was going on for me, and that
helped my entire family also talk about their experiences and
fears. At the end of my father's life, I was with him, so grateful that I had learned to hold myself so I could be with him
as he died.

Here is how it works. The Feeling Chamber is a safe place
to learn how to be with your emotions. In the Feeling Chamber,
you sit quietly, breathe into your heart, and open yourself to the
question, "What am I feeling in this moment?"

It is an act of power to stop exiting the discomfort and to
let yourself enter the Feeling Chamber of your heart. When you
take responsibility for your emotions, you can learn to sit with
them as you would sit with a scared, upset child. For indeed,
your emotions are like little children. Some have been sitting
in the corner, trembling and ashamed after being ignored for
a very long time, like two-year-olds having a messy, loud tantrum. Your role is to go to your heart, get quiet, sit, and let the
feelings come to you.

It can be helpful to visualize an actual room or area that
represents your Feeling Chamber. You might imagine that your
Feeling Chamber is filled with soft pillows and soothing light-
ing, or visualize it as a safe sacred place in the forest. You might

even have a place in your home or out in nature that can be your Feeling Chamber.

Whether you are using your imagination or physically going to a place that feels secure and nourishing, your Feeling Chamber is a place where you do your best to simply feel your emotions, without judging, trying to figure them out, or trying to determine who is to blame. Simply observe. Notice the impact of your emotions. Be curious about the flavor, feeling, and sensations of your emotions.

Explore where you feel the emotions in your body. Emotions are not to be experienced in the mind but in your actual physical form. Here are more questions to ask yourself:

Where am I feeling the emotion in my body?
What else am I feeling?
What is beneath the emotion that I don't want to see?
Is the emotion connected to anything or anywhere else in my body?

In the appendix, I share a list of emotions, which I encourage you to read as you are learning about your emotional body. There are all sorts of subtleties to your emotions that you may miss by *thinking* you know what is going on. But is that really anger burning in your belly, or are you feeling envious or hatred or a sense of being powerless? Is the pressure in your chest connected to the grief of loneliness or despair? Keep refining what the emotion is and how it feels in your body.

Here are the five steps to entering the Feeling Chamber:

1. Close all the exits, the places where you usually go to avoid the emotion.
2. Turn inward and get quiet.

3. Breathe and notice where the emotion lives in your body.

4. Allow the emotion the physical and mental space to arise.

5. Refrain from judging, pushing down, or defending the emotion. Just allow.

Spend at least five minutes in the Feeling Chamber, being with your current emotions. If you need to, set a timer. Or you can call a friend to sit with you either physically or on the phone as you enter into the heart of your Feeling Chamber. Do your best to stay with yourself and not think or exit in other ways. Be with the discomfort. Be with the pain. Be with the fear. Imagine you are sitting with a dying person and bringing all of your grace and compassion as you hold their hand and let them know you are with them.

"Hi, emotional body. I'm here. I see you. I'm listening. What do you have to share with me?"

There is nothing to do. Just be.

Only once you have named, recognized, and sat with the emotion(s), you will move to the second chamber of the heart, the Story Chamber. But I have to warn you, the temptation is to feel the emotion for a nanosecond and then immediately start telling yourself the story. Refrain! Keep going back to what you are feeling in your body.

When you notice that you are thinking or replaying the story, take a big breath. Exhale and come back to your body. Ask your heart to help you stay out of the Story Chamber and rest into the Feeling Chamber. At first, it may be difficult, but with practice, you will learn how to keep the Feeling Chamber and the Story Chamber separated.

## Veronique: Unweaving Rage at Work

Over the past year, I've started getting these intense flashes of anger when I'm at work. I came to a Warrior Heart workshop because the anger felt uncontrollable, and I was afraid I was going to say something I would regret. When I tried to push the rage away, I got terrible headaches and felt exhausted. Nothing seemed to be helping.

Your explanation of the importance of feeling the emotion separate from the story helped me to piece together what was going on. Before when I felt the rage, I would make up a story to justify it—why the other person was making me mad. I would also work even more obsessively to try to bury the feeling. After the workshop, I made the commitment to myself to slow down and to take time to be with the rage.

The next time the anger came, I actually excused myself from a meeting and went and sat in my office with the door closed. I set a timer for five minutes and let the rage come. It was like a volcano exploding in my belly and chest. Instead of thinking about it or trying to attach the feeling to anything, I just stayed with the volcano. About two minutes in, I noticed that there was fear under the volcano. So I put a hand on my low belly and invited the fear in. The fear was connected to a feeling of drowning, that I couldn't keep up. When the timer went off, I felt oddly empty. The rage never came back as intensely, because I had finally paid attention to it and was able to then go into the Story Chamber to see that my need to be perfect was crippling me and causing me to short-circuit. Separating the feeling from the story allowed me to address the story directly once the emotions had cleared and to rec-ognize how my own beliefs were creating the rage, not my coworkers.

## *Healing Your Emotions*

Our culture is moving more and more toward distraction and, in many ways, destruction. The level of violence, suicide, addiction, and injustice all around us is escalating. On the surface, it might look like too many expressed emotions are the cause, but it is the opposite. It is our buried emotions and the detrimental cross-wiring that we have with our emotional body and our stories that cause our society to be under dangerous internal pressure. Anytime something is under pressure, it will find a way to release the tension, often in a dramatic and uncontrollable way.

When we are not clearing out our emotions in a healthy way, we end up perpetrating violence against each other and ourselves. Extreme cases are rape, murder, and suicide. Each of us has been guilty of some degree of violence. Getting furious and angrily blaming a coworker or a friend or a beloved. Road rage. Extreme guilt or shame turned inward. Overeating. Over-working. Overthinking. Pleasing others at the expense of our own well-being. These types of violence to self and others may seem minor taken one at a time, but seen as a whole, we are both the perpetrators and the victims of a great deal of harm.

Our work in learning how to be with our emotions in a new way is crucial to our own well-being and the well-being of everyone around us.

Now, I am *not* inviting you to express your emotions however and whenever you want as a way to release them. This form of dumping your emotions on others is not healthy or beneficial. It creates more drama and hurt and only moves the emotional mess around rather than actually cleaning it up.

And there is a lot of mess we are all currently cleaning up. We are not only cleaning up our own old unprocessed emotional content from our childhood onward but also any emotional messes that our parents inadvertently passed on to us.

Imagine it this way. Let's go back to the image of the backpack filled with all the unexpressed emotions you've accumulated over your lifetime. Part of what you are carrying in your backpack is the overflow of your parents' emotional struggles: your mother's unwillingness to feel her grief at the loss of her first child or your father's repressed fury at his father for sexually abusing him as a child. And it goes beyond this to the burdens your ancestors carried and unwittingly passed on to their descendants.

There is a whole science now being developed called *epigenetics*. Epigenetics is about how trauma is passed down through our genes. So, for example, if your family was in the Holocaust, or if you are fully or partially descended from slaves brought forcefully to the United States, or your grandmother's great-great-aunt was burned at the stake, you also carry the echoes of these traumas. I bring this up not to overwhelm you but to help you get a larger context of the magnitude of cleaning we are inviting you to do and why the desire to bury our heads in the proverbial sand is so compelling.

But do you really want to pass all this down to your children? Do you really want to spend your precious life unsuccessfully fighting to avoid the backpack of your past? Or are you ready for your own liberation?

Be brave, Warrior of the Heart. Your awareness is what heals. You have the immense gift to be in a time when you have the tools, such as the Warrior Heart practice, to finally put down that heavy backpack and clear out the old, heavy past not just for yourself but for all those who came before you and all those who will come after you.

And it doesn't have to be hard or endless. In fact, I invite you to think about it as emotional play rather than emotional work.

Cleaning is cleaning. Whether it is your house, your car, your physical body, or your emotional body, there will always be cleaning to do. You can fight the cleaning or embrace the cleaning—that is your choice. Cleaning your physical body, from brushing your teeth to taking showers to washing your hands, is not a huge chore or burden; it is just something you do. Same with your house. You may not enjoy sweeping your floors or washing the dishes, but you most likely don't want to deal with the consequences of never cleaning your home. It is the same with your emotional body. Emotions stagnate and become stinky, or gather in great piles of heavy energy that constantly trip us when left unattended to. We end up being both bruised and constantly frustrated.

Imagine the sensation of driving your freshly washed and vacuumed car or the sense of spaciousness and ease after you have cleared out your closet or pantry or organized your desk at work. When you learn to clean your emotional body, you'll find you become naturally happier, more loving, and more peaceful. Living with a cluttered emotional body is painful. Tending to your emotional body can be joyful when you look toward the long-term benefits.

This is a long-term process, not a quick fix. While you will often feel better immediately as you work through the Warrior Heart practice, remember that you do not have to (and you really can't) clear out all your old emotional content at once. This process takes time and patience. Work steadily, a little at a time, to clean what is arising in the moment. Keep doing the practice, going through the Feeling, Story, Truth, and Intent Chambers one issue, trigger, or fear at a time.

What are the long-term benefits of emotional clearing? More creativity. A deep sense of peace. Intuitive wisdom. As you turn toward the Feeling Chamber instead of distracting and avoiding your emotions, and as you continue forward to untangle the false beliefs in the Story Chamber, you'll find yourself responding with an open heart and mind to your surroundings rather than reacting and defending.

What also happens as you do your own emotional work is that you become more comfortable with other people's emotions. It is easy to sit and listen to the fear beneath your friend's anger or to stay compassionate and present when your beloved shares a worry. As you learn to be with yourself in the Feeling Chamber and then free yourself of the old stories from the past, all your relationships will improve, because you will be in the present, and others will feel your compassion and steadiness.

You will also find that you have more choice about who and how you interact with people. You'll be able to set boundaries and be more honest about what you want, because with a clearer emotional body, you can feel when someone wants to dump their emotional mess on you or when they are genuinely trying to clean.

## Moving Beyond Resistance

Cleaning up your emotions by following the Warrior Heart practice, starting with the Feeling Chamber, is a three-step process. (1) Stop exiting your emotions. (2) Turn toward the discomfort. (3) Be with what you are feeling without analyzing, judging, or trying to change anything. But there may be a lot of resistance that arises. Here are some ways to navigate the challenges.

### FEAR

Being a Heart Warrior doesn't mean you will not have fear. Fear is not a sign that something is wrong; it is a sign that something needs your attention. Your mind might tell you all sorts of stories about why you should not go into the Feeling Chamber.

Here are some of the main fears that I hear:

1. If I let myself feel that feeling, I won't be able to stop.
2. I'll hurt someone terribly if I actually feel my rage.
3. I'm afraid to revisit a painful memory and get hurt again.
4. I don't know what else will be unleashed if I open the door to my emotions.

There can be a fear that you'll somehow be annihilated or be completely abandoned if you go into the emotion.

Go slow. Never push or force yourself into the Feeling Chamber. You want to adopt the attitude of inviting your emotions to join you as you sit and experience and observe them. You can imagine that you are dipping your toe into cold water; start small and stay with yourself, and over time, you will find that you can swim in those dark depths while breathing through your fear.

Since it is often the child part of us that didn't know how to process the old emotions, we can experience nonrational animal fear at the thought of going back to those past feelings. For support, I've found it can be helpful to find something that represents your child-self. Spend a few days interacting with this representation of your child-self; talk to it, carry it around, soothe it. Your rational mind may feel silly interacting with your ancient teddy bear or a basketball or a recently purchased stuffed animal, but your inner child-self will start feeling safer that there is an adult present. Then when you go into the Feeling Chamber, hold your child-self (Little Soul) and invite that part of you to cry, rage, or tremble.

Remember: "What do you need, sweetheart? What are you feeling? I'm right here. . . ." Let the emotions flow and pay attention.

### PAST TRAUMA

If you experienced physical, emotional, sexual, or verbal abuse in your childhood, or any situation that resulted in disassociation or post-traumatic stress disorder, please be extra mindful when using the Warrior Heart practice. Since trauma is stored in the body, you may need to find extra support from someone who specializes in somatic counseling. More specialized resources are listed in the appendix.

If you notice yourself disassociating, going numb, going blank, or getting caught in a traumatic memory, put one hand on your heart and one hand on your belly, and gently bring yourself back into the present. Stand up and stomp your feet on the ground. Shake your body from head to toe. Make noise. It is really important that you not retraumatize yourself, which will only deepen the wounding. There is a way to experience past trauma and clear it, and it takes extra care and gentleness with yourself to do this. See more about working with trauma in the appendix.

## Trish: Healing Trauma

I was sexually abused by a neighbor as a child, and while I thought that I had somehow grown out of it, I soon discovered through the Warrior Heart work that I had more healing to do. Because I started to get curious about the difference between my emotions and my story, I noticed that whenever I was around new people, I would go between feeling numb and feeling anxious. It was so familiar that I didn't even notice it. My body had never forgotten that it was a stranger who abused me, and it equated new people with abuse.

Instead of pretending I was okay, I started paying attention to the little signs that my body was in freeze mode. I did this by really consciously talking with people I didn't know for a couple of minutes (at the grocery store or café), and then I'd go sit by myself and notice how I felt. If I felt numb, I'd stomp my feet or sing out loud in the car, anything to get myself back in the present. If I went into flight mode, I'd stay with the feeling of panic and needing to run away to be safe. What worked best was putting one hand on my heart and one hand on my belly and reminding myself I was safe. It was my own willingness and the support of friends and my therapist that helped me to rewire my emotional body so I no longer panicked around people I didn't know.

Here are some other things to pay attention to when you are working with your emotions:

## DISTRACTION

Some people find it nearly impossible to go into the Feeling Chamber without being hooked by 101 distractions. When an emotion arises, notice if you have a habit of suddenly finding something else vitally important to do. Do your best to minimize distractions when you are stepping into the Feeling Chamber. Put your phone on airplane mode, turn off your computer, and let others know that you are busy so that you are not interrupted. It can also help to put your hands on your heart and belly and breathe slowly to ground you in your body when you notice you are being hooked by distractions.

## PROJECTION

*Projection* is a psychological defense mechanism in which individuals attribute characteristics they find unacceptable in themselves and project them onto another person. If you find yourself saying, "I don't have any anger, but my husband/mother/boss needs to deal with their issues!" or "I hate it when others cry; they are just being victims," you may be projecting your own unprocessed emotional content onto others. Watch for where you may be projecting your words and thoughts rather than owning what you are actually feeling.

## NUMBNESS

If you were taught to never have emotions or if emotions were never expressed in your family, it may seem daunting to get in touch with what you are feeling. As someone who used to numb out emotions, I found it really helpful to talk to my emotional body and give myself permission to feel. Over time, as you patiently tune into your emotions, they will begin to break through the shell of protective numbness. Don't judge yourself with what you think you should be feeling or experiencing; just be gentle and open.

### SPINNING

If you have an emotion that you keep cycling over and over again, you are probably caught in a spin cycle. This is usually because you have tangled up a story and an emotion so thoroughly that they are locked in a wrestlers' embrace. Usually the story that is presenting as the cause of the emotion is only the surface story with a deeper, older story that is actually keeping the spin going. Ask a friend or a therapist to help you go beneath the current story to explore what childhood experience or belief is not allowing you to clear the emotion.

Step-by-step, as you face rather than avoid the emotional debris that has accumulated over the years of avoidance and stuffing feelings away, you'll find you have more energy and enthusiasm. Remember, this is a long-term process. You'll be coming back to the Feeling Chamber over and over again, so settle in for a long-term relationship with your emotional body.

Now that you are familiar with the Feeling Chamber and you are learning to turn toward rather than away from difficult emotions, you are ready to move into the Story Chamber. Bring your warrior spirit and your open heart; it is time to do some major inner untangling.

# *Review*

You enter the Warrior Heart practice by learning to gently sit with emotional triggers, fears, or pain that arises within you, *separate from the story* you believe is causing the emotion. In the Feeling Chamber, the goal is not to fix, understand, or explain emotions but to simply be with them consciously.

### Feeling Chamber Questions

- What am I feeling?
- How does it affect my physical body?
- Where do I feel closed, and where do I feel open?
- How can I support myself in staying open to my discomfort?
- When was the last time I felt this same emotion?
- Is there another emotion beneath this one?
- What is this emotion trying to tell me?

The keys to unlocking the Feeling Chamber are your breath and your presence.

When an intense emotion arises, you can best support yourself by staying in the present moment, getting curious about where you are feeling the emotion in your body, and increasing the length of your inhale and exhale. Often when we want to avoid our emotions, we start breathing shallowly, or we even hold our breath, which only makes matters worse. Keep talking to yourself as you would talk to a scared or overwhelmed child, breathing into your belly. It is also often helpful to put a hand on your belly or heart or breathe into your feet to help you stay in the present moment.

# Feeling Chamber Exercises

### Your Feeling Chamber

Imagine your Feeling Chamber as an actual space. What does your Feeling Chamber look like? Use your imagination to build in the details of what your Feeling Chamber looks like. Is it dark or light, inside or outside, soft or hard, big or small? What colors and textures are part of your Feeling Chamber? Close your eyes and visualize your Feeling Chamber, or write about it. You can also make a painting or a collage or find a picture on the internet or in a magazine that best reflects your Feeling Chamber.

### Journaling

Every morning, take three minutes to write out what you are feeling. Don't edit or justify; simply let yourself free-form write, being curious about what your emotional body has to share with you through words or pictures.

### Body Scan

Several times during the day, sit quietly for two minutes and ask yourself, *What sensations am I feeling right now?* Close your eyes and turn your gaze inside. Take a couple of slow, deep breaths. Now explore the physical sensations in your body. Where are you tight? Where do you feel relaxed? What do your feet feel like against the floor? What is the sensation of the air on your skin? How do your shoulders feel? How about your pelvis and hips? Notice as much as you can about your inner experience. Don't try to change anything; simply pay attention.

Now observe the emotions moving through you. Do you

feel frustrated, scared, irritated, joyful? What is the quality of these emotions, and how do you sense them in your body? Are they hot or cold, heavy or light, tense or bubbly? Also explore where you feel these emotions. Is your stomach tight with a sense of worry and dread, or are you grinding your teeth together in frustration or anger? Name everything you can, locating the sensation and qualities of the emotions in your body.

Set a timer for two (or more) minutes if it will help you. Stay dedicated to simply watching without interfering with what is happening in your physical and emotional body.

Keep practicing the body scan regularly throughout your day. It only takes thirty seconds to go within. Start at your feet and take a breath. Then let your awareness travel up your body, taking in the information about your current physical sensations and emotional experience.

If you want, you can keep a journal to write down what you discover.

Making the body scan a daily practice will help you get more familiar with your emotional body and make it easier to check in with yourself when you are stressed or upset.

### Emotional Literacy

Often we either ignore our emotions or make broad generalizations to describe what we are feeling, instead of listening to the fine details of our inner landscape. Regularly review the list of emotions in the appendix. It can also be really helpful to print the list of emotions out and hang them on your fridge or tape them to your bathroom mirror so you see them often. Now when you express the broad strokes of "I'm sad" or "I'm upset," take time to fill in the finer details of what you are feeling.

Naming the subtleties of your emotions gives you more clarity and more power to sit with them.

### Emotional Fluidity

In his book *Emotions Revealed,* researcher Paul Ekman shares how he discovered that all humans, regardless of culture or age, express emotions through their face in exactly the same way. What that means is that there are distinct facial expressions for disgust, or delight, or shock that are universal to all humans. He further found that by learning how to contract or relax your facial muscles, you can show and stimulate the different emotions.

I've found it helpful to practice in the mirror making different facial expressions to see and begin to feel different emotions. What does fear look like on your face? How about shock or envy? Try out different facial expressions and see how this allows you to begin to feel the emotion in your body. Switch back and forth between different emotions, practicing becoming more fluid. Go into one emotion 100 percent, then bring your face back to neutral and switch to another emotion. If you have a frozen emotional body, this will help to thaw your emotions so they become more accessible. If you tend to get stuck in an emotion, this will help you learn to switch between different states.

### The Vertical Drop

This vertical drop exercise is modified from the book *Undefended Love.*

The goal of the vertical drop is to ask and answer questions—engaging in self-inquiry—until we discover something about ourselves that we didn't know before we started. When properly done, the process ends with a feeling of open relaxation and wonderment.

To do the vertical drop (with yourself or with a friend), use the image of slowly climbing down a ladder. As you take each step down the ladder, you are journeying further into your emotion awareness. At each step, you ask yourself (or your friend asks you) a question to help you go deeper.

Because often the emotion that is presenting itself is only the tip of the iceberg, the vertical drop helps us to explore what other emotions are also stirred up within us.

The best questions invite us to slow down, to listen, and to feel.

At the top rung of the ladder, you start with, "What am I feeling?"

Pause and name the feeling. Just be with it. Breathe.

And what is underneath that feeling?

Imagine you are taking a step down the ladder. Imagine you are going another step into your emotional body.

Don't try to rush the answer or force anything. Just hang out on that next step, listening and waiting. Keep asking, "What is underneath that feeling?"

Stay with yourself as you go down the ladder, counting each step as you discover a new layer on your journey of going deeper into unknown territory.

## 4

# The Story Chamber

*Your pain is the breaking of the shell that*
*encloses your understanding.*

—Kahlil Gibran

ONE OF THE BONUSES of getting a divorce in my late forties was the awkward adult terror of dating in my early fifties for the first time in decades. After three men I dated chose to be with younger women, I gave myself a good talking-to in order to keep from spinning out into a horror story around aging and desirability.

Once I caught my mind mush-ing (one of my favorite terms, learned from a Unity minister while I was on a book tour long ago: **Making Up Sh\*t**), I went right into the Warrior Heart practice.

As I sat in the Feeling Chamber, I was startled to realize I felt ashamed to be dating. Ashamed to be a divorcée. Ashamed that I was probably doing it wrong, and especially ashamed that I chose to be in relationships with men who didn't reciprocate. I felt exposed, naked, and way too vulnerable. That shame was in turn fueling a story that I was broken, that no one would want me, and that I should just give up and resign myself to being an elderly spinster who had a lot of cats waiting at home for her. (Oh, except I'm allergic to cats. Damn.) "There is no hope!" my story said. "See, we have the evidence. No one wants you. Stop embarrassing yourself by trying."

You are probably very familiar with the Story Chamber and its drama, as it is where most of us spend a lot of our precious time.

In my imagination, the Story Chamber is like a huge unkempt library run by a pair of terrible twins, Julie the Judge and Victor the Victim. Julie is thin and nervous and has the mind of a lawyer on too much coffee. She is always ready to share her opinion and prove her point. Victor is slow, a little clumsy, and constantly placating his sister. He apologizes all the time and wants everyone to like him.

When something goes wrong, Julie starts pulling out books and reading lists and lists of Victor's past mistakes, or she writes new volumes of terrible things that might happen in their future. It is always Victor's fault, and he knows it. No matter how much he tries to appease Julie, he feels hopeless and lost. And no matter how much she tries to control their lives, she is always resentful. . . .

We all have an inner Julie and Victor, two parts of us that are at war. Anytime you blame or criticize yourself or another, worry about the future, or fret about the past, you are allying with Julie the Judge. And anytime you feel ashamed and hopeless because you are never good enough or that the world is against you, you are allying with Victor the Victim. There are never any winners in this inner battle, only a lot of collateral damage to your body, mind, and self-esteem.

As a Warrior of the Heart, you are learning to align with

a new ally: your witness-self. It will take time to shift your attention from believing your Julie and Victor selves. Remember they are really convincing, especially when they have hijacked your emotions with their stories of doom and gloom. But you are stronger. All you need is your warrior awareness and your heart curiosity to guide you. It's time to step into the mess of your mind and reclaim your Warrior Heart power.

## *Stepping into the Messy Mind*

Your mind is usually a messy, chaotic place filled with not only the voices of your own personal Julie and Victor but also the differing opinions of your mother, father, teachers, friends, peers, partners, and the society you were raised in. It can get really busy in there!

From an early age, we take all these voices and opinions and all our experiences, good and bad, and start crafting our very own story. We are great storytellers, and soon we have decided who we are and how we should behave. We also have a list of rules about who others should be and how they should behave, as well as a list of rules of how the world should be.

Over time, we add to our inner rule book, but we rarely remove any rules. As you can imagine, Julie the Judge loves the rule book, but as there are more and more rules, some of which begin to contradict each other, she can get more and more frantic trying to keep the order. Victor the Victim takes the brunt of her frustration and feels more and more helpless and ashamed.

We try harder and harder to be "good" or "productive" or "smart" and follow the rules, but this takes us further and further away from who we really are. As we have more experiences, both beautiful and challenging, we weave more and more stories that imprison us with what was, what could have been, and what should be.

We also take on specific roles that we use as a template to fit who we think we should be. So, for example, we might take on the role in our story of the Martyr Mother, or the Busy-Bee Businessperson, or the Youngest Neglected Child.

The mind might be a messy place with all our rules, stories, and roles, but our stories and roles also give us a sense of safety. Let's go back to our model of Big Soul and Little Soul.

When your Big Soul and Little Soul are connected, you have little need for elaborate stories; you're too busy enjoying life. But when your Little Soul is disconnected from your Big Soul, then your Little Soul creates all sorts of elaborate stories and detailed roles that it clings to for a sense of identity and purpose.

Front and center of your Little Soul, which is created by many different voices and opinions, is Julie the Judge and/or Victor the Victim. And oooh, do they both love stories. Couple your ego-personality's different selves writing dramatic novel-like stories with a cocktail of repressed or stirred emotions, and you have a potent recipe for suffering.

As one of my students said, "It's a mess in there."

But the mess can be cleaned through the Warrior Heart practice.

When I was first developing the Warrior Heart practice, I initially called the four chambers *the four rooms*. Whenever one of us was confused or upset by something, my friend Sarah and I would have great fun saying to each other, "Go to your room!" Which meant, of course, "Do the Warrior Heart practice!"

Please remember that the gift of the Warrior Heart practice

is learning to separate out each of the four different chambers: Feeling from Story, Story from Truth, and then getting clarity on your Intent. Be systematic, and don't skip chambers or try to move quickly through them. Just as the heart needs all four chambers to function properly, you need the patience and perseverance to train yourself in attending to each chamber distinctly.

The first chamber, the Feeling Chamber, is about learning to be with your emotions. The second chamber, the Story Chamber, is about learning to be with and witnessing your stories.

The initial question of the Story Chamber is: "What am I telling myself?" And just like the Feeling Chamber, you want to explore not just the surface but be willing to go into the depths of your story. This means being super honest with yourself about what is going on in your mind and what you are actually telling yourself. This is important. Be aware of defaulting to what you think your story should be or what you wish your story were.

The only way through is to settle in and really witness what is happening in your Story Chamber.

Your witness-self is the part of you that has no opinions or attachment to the story. Witness-self simply sees what is happening in your Story Chamber without judgment or justification. When you enter into your Story Chamber to observe, you do so without trying to make the story better or worse. Do your best to notice how you experience the story in your body and to be curious about how the story is triggering your emotional body.

Pretend you are a detective, and you have all the information you need in the Story Chamber to understand why you are struggling or confused. But remember that the "facts" that make up your story are not truths; what your story claims to be truths are mostly lies or misrepresentations of the truth.

As with the Feeling Chamber, the attitude you want to bring to the Story Chamber is curiosity, compassion, and a whole lot of witness.

## Peter: Late Friend

She said she would call me in the afternoon, and by 7:00 p.m., I still hadn't heard from her. I noticed myself increasingly worrying, checking my phone repeatedly, and making up stories about what had happened. I stopped everything and sat in meditation for a few minutes. Then I started the Warrior Heart practice.

At first, the emotions and the story were all mixed together: "She is mad at me. I did something wrong." I felt like a bad person. I imagined myself entering deeper into the Feeling Chamber and went toward the feeling of being a bad person. There was a familiar drowning feeling, a sense of despair. I realized I felt lost and confused, like a little kid. I didn't know what I had done wrong, but I felt I was in trouble and there was nothing I could do.

The story then became so clear: I was linking my friend not calling me with my history of my mother not talking to me when she was mad. The false story said: If she hasn't called me, it is because I did something wrong and she is punishing me.

I saw the truth was that all I really knew was that my friend hadn't called me. And that my intent was to stay open. A few hours later, she called me, apologizing that her phone battery had died. In the past, I would have been so busy projecting my mother onto her that I would have brought all my old hurt and upset. Instead, I was able to be openhearted with her.

You can explore the connection between your story and your emotions, but try to stay focused on staying in the Story Chamber rather than going back to the Feeling Chamber. At the end of the Warrior Heart practice, we will revisit the Feeling Chamber, but for now, you want to immerse yourself in the world of your story. You may find that the story you are telling yourself is causing a negative emotion or that the initial story you find is actually hiding a deeper fear.

### Here Are Five Specific Steps to Entering the Story Chamber:

1. Let go of trying to do it "right." Be willing to get messy.
2. Turn inward and get quiet.
3. Allow all the layers of the story to present themselves.
4. Breathe and notice what the effect of the story is in your body and life.
5. Refrain from judging, pushing down, or defending the story. Just witness.

Spend at least five minutes in the Story Chamber being with your inner dialogue and thoughts. Set a timer if this helps you stay focused. You can also use your journal to write without editing as a means of entering into the Story Chamber. Do your best to stay with yourself and try not to make a better story or exit in other ways. Be with the mess. Be with the judgment and fear. Be with the little kid victim voice. Imagine you are sitting with a child having a tantrum, simply witnessing the explosion of words and sounds. *Hello, my mind. I'm here. I'm listening. What do you have to share with me? Don't hold anything back.*

If you notice that you are going blank or trying to avoid parts of your story, take a big breath. Exhale and then drop into your body. Ask your heart to help you stay in the Story Chamber and unearth everything that is there to be brought to the light. At first, it may seem awkward, but with practice, you will learn how to stay steady so you can keep delving deeper into the Story Chamber.

Keep asking the questions: *What am I telling myself about this situation? What is actually going on in my mind?* Pay attention to the voices that say, *I shouldn't have this story,* or *I thought I was done with this story. What is wrong with me?* Watch out for the ways your mind will try to make you wrong for having your story: *Why am I still judging people?* or *I should be more loving!*

Also, don't try to jump forward to figure out what the truth is yet. Just allow yourself to be in the jumbly mess of the story. As you come to sit and observe your story, you'll find more and more layers of fiction, some that you wrote a long time ago and some that may not even be your story.

## *Experiencing It All*

When you enter into the Story Chamber without your usual defenses and justifications, it is like you are walking into the wilderness of your inner landscape. Bring your witness-self to the Story Chamber and imagine you can walk among the trees that represent your different stories, taking in both the individual trees and the entire forest.

Sometimes going into the Story Chamber, your first inclination is to try to clean it up. Resist! Let it be messy. When we allow the fullness of the mess to unfold and witness it in all of its glory, only then we can get to the roots of the issue.

Here is how it goes. I'm exploring the thoughts and narrative in my Story Chamber around dating and my fear of being an old spinster who will never be partnered again. As I keep digging, I notice that there is a deeper story that I must be in a relationship to be a "good" person. "If I'm in a relationship, then I'm wanted, which means I'm valuable, which means I'm worthy."

Ah, now I'm getting to a younger part of myself. That's good.

It may feel scary, or distasteful, or annoying to uncover childlike/young agreements in your Story Chamber—especially when you want to be a groovy, together adult. But if you want to be a groovy, together adult, that means you must face the judge-victim fun house of your Little Soul trying to stay safe in a hall of distorted mirrors and fairy tales. You don't want to get lost in the carnival or cowered by the barking voices. You do want to witness, and really see, what you are doing to yourself inside your clever little head.

If you try to make your thoughts nicer or more spiritual, you are only letting yourself stay on the surface of your story. Just like with the Feeling Chamber, it takes tremendous bravery to stay and witness what your mind is actually doing. It takes courage to face yourself, to turn away from Facebook, to turn away from your image of perfection, to turn away from who you think you are supposed to be and instead to turn toward your raw, primitive, and chaotic mind.

Simply start naming what you are perceiving in the Story Chamber. *Yes, here I am, judging myself. Here I am, hating that other person. Here I am, wishing I were different. Here I am, wanting him to hurt as badly as I do.* Be honest. Say it all, no filters, no editing.

If you find you are judging yourself for your drama, or feeling victimized by it, pause. Take a breath in. Exhale slowly. Ask for help from your inner wisdom to reconnect you to your witness so that you can observe your story without believing it 100 percent. Can you allow even just 10 percent of yourself to observe the story line?

You'll often be surprised by what you find, and that is really the best attitude to have when going into the Story Chamber: wonder. As in, *I wonder what I have created in my head. . . .* You'll probably find a whole mix of thoughts and stories, not just from the present but also from the past—from your parents, from movies, and from your own creative wackiness.

My favorite is when I discover something in the Story Chamber that I didn't realize I was thinking (but is totally affecting/infecting my reality). For example, when I was exploring my stories around dating, what I eventually discovered was a very old fairy-tale belief that I could only be happy if I were in an intimate relationship. (Cue, "And they lived happily ever after!" and "Riding into the sunset.") My mind had been telling me I should be in a partnership—and if I wasn't, I should be suffering and feeling bad about myself. The moment I saw that story line, I started laughing, because I realized I was happy and content with my life as it was and that the story was the only thing making me unhappy, not being single.

Your story often seems logical, or the "right" way to think on the surface, but if you explore it more, you will find the flaws in your thinking. There is no one way to be happy, and whether you are in a relationship or not, or have a certain job, or a specific amount of money in the bank has no relevance on your self-worth. Watch out for any place your mind is telling you that you "should" be some way, because that is a surefire sign that it is lying to you. There are no shoulds.

The greatest support I can give to you around the Story Chamber is in learning to love your stories and your experiences. Be amazed by how creative, resilient, and powerful you are. Your stories are not inherently good or bad. Remember, you are not trying to get rid of your stories or pretend your life challenges never happened. You are learning, with your presence and compassion, to face your stories straight on—the judgment, the victimization, and the suffering they can bring.

## Growing Your Awareness

The purpose of working separately with each chamber is to create space between your emotions and thoughts, and your thoughts and the truth. After you do the practice a few times, you'll find yourself more easily untangling confusion and finding clarity. What will also start to happen is that you'll grow something that is critical to personal freedom: your awareness.

As we talked about in the introduction, most of us live without awareness, bouncing between the Feeling and the Story Chambers, attempting to use our stories to completely avoid or fiercely justify our feelings. Without awareness, we are at the mercy of our old agreements and beliefs, and our stories are living us rather than us consciously choosing our stories.

Awareness brings you into the present and gives you the

courage to unearth all of your buried emotions and stories. You can begin to sort what you want to keep and what you want to release when they are no longer hidden. Instead of your emotions and stories being who you are, you recognize your emotions and stories are often products of your thinking, which then gives you the power to change your perspective. Awareness, or being able to consciously witness what you are feeling and what we are thinking, is your greatest ally.

As your awareness expands, so does the space around your emotions and stories. Where previously your Feeling and Story Chambers might have been cramped and dimly lit with the shallowness of your awareness, you now find yourself in an open expanse, able to see your feelings and stories from many different angles. Instead of immediately reacting to other people or situations, you'll find you have the room between your emotions and thoughts to make new choices and take new actions.

## *Sarina: A New Relationship with Mom*

*One of my students wrote when she discovered her witness-self:*

I'm having an incredible experience with my mom. Instead of reacting to her in the same way I always have, I'm witnessing Sarina being triggered by her mother, almost like I'm watching it from the outside rather than the inside. Since I'm able to witness our interactions, I'm not responding in the same habitual way. It feels weird but also amazingly freeing. This is also helping me to explore the story I've created in great detail and realize how much of it is untrue.

In the Story Chamber, your first job is to be an archeologist, digging up the buried stories of your past and bringing them into the light where you can study and catalog them. Later, you will learn how to take action, allowing you to transform your perspective. For now, be disciplined when you visit the Story Chamber to unearth and dust off the story lines of your past, fully present, with a shovel of awareness and fine brush of compassion.

Once you've laid the story out before you, it's time to move to the next chamber, the Truth Chamber. Now let's explore the fine art of fully stepping out of the Story and into the Truth. (It's both more difficult and easier than you think!)

## *Review*

### Story Chamber Questions

- What am I telling myself?
- What words have I woven together?
- What old agreements and rules are embedded in my story?
- How can I support myself in listening to a deeper layer of this story?
- How old is this story? How long have I been telling it to myself?
- Are there any parts of this story that I have picked up from other people, that are not even my story?

The keys to opening the Story Chamber are willingness and permission.

You must be willing to witness your mind and be honest about what you are telling yourself. Give yourself permission to write out in great detail in your journal, or speak about your story with someone who is neutral and can help be a mirror so you can clearly see what you are telling yourself.

## Story Chamber Exercises

### Your Story Chamber

You can imagine your Story Chamber as an actual space, just like you did with the Feeling Chamber. What does your Story Chamber look like? As I mentioned before, mine is a disheveled library with lots and lots of books crammed on the shelves. It always feels busy in my Story Chamber. But yours might be all straight lines and narrow hallways, like a huge circus tent filled with performers, or more akin to a board of directors meeting. Close your eyes and visualize your Story Chamber, or write about it. You can also make a painting or a collage, or find a picture on the internet or in a magazine that best reflects your Story Chamber.

### Journaling

Every morning, take three minutes to write out whatever is in your thoughts. Don't edit or justify; simply let yourself free-form write, being curious about what your mind has to share with you through words or pictures.

### Acting Out Your Story

Sometimes the only way to truly enter the story fully is to act it out, either in your head or with your body.

To act out the story in your mind, use your imagination to

go back to the incident you are working with. Let's say that you had a fight with a friend. After you sit in the Feeling Chamber and have tracked your emotions (perhaps frustration, disappointment, and resignation), imagine the exact fight you had with them. Then, in your mind's eye, call up the location, how you were feeling at the time, and what words were exchanged. Bring in as much detail as you can.

Now imagine that you can step back and watch the interaction between you and your friend, and listen to the dialogue between you. Ask yourself the following as you observe these two humans interact: *Is there a deeper story line being triggered here? What was I thinking at the time? What story am I telling myself now?*

Don't force the information to come; just allow the story to bubble up. Be attentive and listen carefully to what you were thinking at the time and what you are thinking about the event now.

Another way to access the story is to physically act it out. Imagine you are a great actor that can enact your role and your friend's role in the drama between you. Speak out loud and gesture fully, even exaggerating your interaction. You can explore both sides by also becoming the person you were fighting with. As you play both roles, make sure a part of you is witnessing and paying close attention to the underlying story that is being acted out.

There are many ways to engage in your story; these examples are just two. You can also journal, use dolls or stuffed animals to act out the scenes, or call a friend (one that will ask you good questions!) to outwardly process so you can be supported in witnessing your story. Be creative. Be curious. Be compassionate.

### Organizing Your Stories

When I was studying home and office organization, I learned a helpful trick: Go through everything you own and find a specific place for it to live. Then, when everything has its place, it is easy to clean because you know immediately where each particular thing goes.

In this same way, you can start to organize your stories so they each have their own place. Just like you will begin to recognize themes of emotions and where they are located in your body when you are in the Feeling Chamber, you will learn to witness your stories as distinct expressions of your mind. Don't try to fix or change them; simply watch the power of the story, where it lives in your body, and how it interacts with other stories. You can create a "map" of your stories and how they connect, or draw pictures, or even create a spreadsheet. Be creative and curious.

# 5

# The Truth Chamber

*Truth is not something outside to be discovered,*
*it is something inside to be realized.*

—Osho

ONE MID-JULY MORNING several years ago, I looked at
my business bank account and went from observing to
panic at a glance. The amount of money I expected to be available in the account was nowhere near what I had thought. We
had just completed some of our biggest events ever; where had
the money gone?

Now, finances and budgeting and all things concerning
numbers have always been a weakness of mine (my eighth-grade
math teacher kindly told me, "I think you should stick with
writing. . . ."). While I can totally geek out on creating spread-
sheets and working in short spurts in QuickBooks, my idea of
financial planning at that time was to look at the bank account
every couple of months and make sure we had money in the
bank. And when we did, I was always delighted and surprised.
"Look, money!"

So when I looked at my account and there was very little

money, I freaked out. My illusion had been that since we had just completed two sold-out journeys to Mexico, we should be fine for a bit. A quick search showed me that we would not be able to afford payroll in a couple of weeks and that there was no source of money coming in for a couple of months.

Fear descended on me like a thunderstorm. My mind started hydroplaning, skidding off the road of reason into worst-case-scenario hyperdrive crash.

I was going to have to fire people and do all these huge amounts of work myself. I was going to have to sell my car. I was going to be homeless—and friendless because I was such a loser. I was never going to be able to finish my next book because I would be begging on the streets.

Then the oh-so-helpful judge started making the case against me.

"You are terrible with money. You've always been terrible with money, see? [Mind shows images of every past financial fiasco and misstep.] You have buried your head in the sand, and now you'll have to pay the price of not doing everything yourself and thinking you can trust others. And you can't trust yourself, so you are basically screwed. No matter how hard you try, you are never going to succeed, you are always going to struggle, and you'll have to close down your business (again) and start over from scratch. You should be better with money. What is wrong with you that you can't take care of something so simple? You are a terrible role model. You call yourself an empowered woman? You call yourself a warrior goddess? You can't even—"

Luckily, in the middle of this tirade, an inner voice cut through the noise and asked me softly, "What is actually true?"

I gently applied the brake and brought my mind to a halt.

I took a breath.

And I stepped out of the Story Chamber and into the Truth Chamber.

The truth is simple.

But getting to the truth can be challenging.

Most of us spend our days going back and forth between the Feeling and Story Chambers, wrestling with the pain and drama of our story and our emotions. We don't know that there are two other chambers waiting and available to help us completely transform how we perceive our reality.

When you live only from the Feeling and Story Chambers, all your experiences are based on your past or an imagined future. You bounce between them, trying to avoid re-creating the pain of your past or worrying about the possible disasters of the future. All your responses are rooted in old unhealed emotional wounds and fears.

The Feeling and Story Chambers are within the domain of your Little Soul. In these two areas, your Little Soul is an expert. It knows the rules and feels safe in the structure it has created. Even though your Little Soul basically lives in a very limited bunker, the huge walls it has created to hold the emotions and the story in place are familiar and comforting (in a painful, cramped sort of way).

Imagine that the Feeling and Story Chambers are two well-protected rooms in an isolated basement of a house. There are very few windows that peek out to the surface, and mostly it is dark and moist and cramped. Someone living in these two rooms exclusively would adapt to the feeling of being held by the confined space and would do their best to keep rearranging the furniture to make themselves more comfortable. There would be places they would avoid, restricting their movement, but they would adjust to the inferior living situation. They would adjust at first because they didn't know there was anything else, and later because it feels like a safe harbor in a scary world.

This is why we cling to our old stories and that sense of being wrapped in a well-worn blanket that brings us comfort and a sense of the known.

For someone who has spent their life making the Story Chamber comfortable and cozy, stepping out into the unknown can be disorienting. Suddenly, there is nothing to grasp onto, nothing for the mind to comfort us with, like saying, "I know how this goes. I know the story. I understand." That's why what most of us do when we step into the Truth Chamber is to immediately rewrite another story and call it the truth.

Instead of actually stepping out of the Story Chamber, our tendency is to drag a piece of the old story with us and then use that as a basis for a new and "better" story. We feel a little bit of relief because we are out of the mess of the Story Chamber, but we still haven't left it behind.

So how do we actually get to the truth? And what is actually true?

## Going Beyond Your Story

*Nothing you believe is true.*
*Knowing this is freedom.*

—BYRON KATIE

The question of the Truth Chamber is this: "What is true?"

Anytime you use more than one sentence to describe the truth, you are back to telling yourself a story.

If you justify, embellish, or explain, you are telling yourself a story.

Commas, semicolons, or run-ons in your sentence? Story.

The truth is simple.

One sentence. Period. Breathe.

But not all one sentences will be the truth. Remember, your mind is tricky and wants to hang on to the story like an old familiar blanket with ratty edges.

When I stepped into the Truth Chamber to explore what was true around my finances after I discovered the low balance, I heard, "You are terrible with money."

As I sat with this sentence, I quickly realized it was a story trying to dress up as the truth.

How could I tell? Because it made me feel bad about myself and want to head back into the Story Chamber to find more evidence.

So I took another breath and asked myself, "What is actually true?"

*My bank balance is less than what I expected it to be.* True.

*Ever since I started my company, we have had enough money in the bank each month to pay our bills.* True.

*We may not have enough money to pay our bills this month.* True.

Now, at this point, my mind wanted to flee back into the Story Chamber and have a disaster mind party. I firmly said, "No, little mind, stay here. Stay in the truth."

"Okay. What else is true?" I asked myself. "Why don't we have money this month?"

Ah yes.

*We paid two years of back taxes and did a complete overhaul on our website.* True.

*I had made the decision to teach much less that year to work on my writing.* True.

"See!!! What a disaster! You should never have taken off time. You have to keep working hard to keep everything afloat! You are responsible for other people's lives, and you are letting them down! You don't get to rest. See what happens! Now your dreams are never going to come true! You always have to be in control and pushing to make sure everything—"

"Come back, my mind. Back to the truth."

Breathe. Get still. Listen. "What else is true?"

*I can borrow money if necessary.* True.

*I can sell something if necessary.* True.

*There are always ebbs and flows in business.* True.

And with that last statement, my whole body relaxed. I remembered that my self-worth is not tied to how much money is in the bank or how many people I support. Running a business is often about juggling and getting through tight times in creative ways. I didn't need to panic or judge myself. I just needed to make an action plan to get us through the crisis at hand and then look at how to make sure it didn't happen again.

True.

When you arrive at a truth, you will notice a sense of spacious ease in your body. It may not immediately feel better than your story, but you will feel an openness within you.

Naming what is true for me, after being caught in the spin of a story, feels like a bell being struck in the center of my being and rippling out, clearing all other thoughts. I am transported out of the drama and upset of the story and into a realm of clarity. This is true. Period.

But your story is going to do its best to reach its tendrils into the Truth Chamber and try to weave another story to obscure the truth. Watch for signs of your story attempting to reassert itself. The biggest sign is that you are thinking and trying to figure things out.

How do you know what the truth is? Learning to home in on the truth takes practice and a diligence in stepping out of your story and how you perceive it.

What you need in abundance is your willingness. Your willingness to step out of the Story Chamber into the Truth Chamber. Your willingness to be wrong (about your story). Your willingness to seek the truth.

A friend once asked me, "But how do I find the willingness?"

One of the main ways to cultivate willingness is to change your self-talk. If you are constantly thinking, *I can't do this,* or *I'm stuck and I don't know what to do next,* or *Nothing ever works out for me,* you are not creating space for your life to change.

Think about the baby who is willing to fall down over and over again as she learns to walk. If the baby weren't willing to fall, she would never try to learn to walk. But a baby's wide-eyed curiosity and strong desire to literally stand up into her potential make every fall a learning experience. The baby is motivated, which leads to willingness. And she doesn't worry about how long it will take to learn to walk; she is simply willing to practice, over and over again.

What is your motivation to get to the truth? For most of us, our motivation is to stop the pain we are experiencing.

### Three Steps to Finding Your Willingness

I. Notice your own suffering and how your mind is causing you pain.

2. Let go of needing to know the answer or understand how to do it.

3. Make mistakes and learn from them (fall down, get up!).

My favorite absolute truth, which you can always count on, is this: "I am breathing."

Say that to yourself right now. "I am breathing." Then take in a deep inhale and release a deep exhale.

There, you are now in the Truth Chamber.

The moment your mind starts talking again (which will be approximately one-half of a second for most of us!), take another breath. "I am breathing."

After several breaths, introduce the question for the Truth Chamber:

"What do I know is true?"

Don't try to force an answer; let the truth arise from the depths of your being.

Remember, the truth is simple.

"What do I know is true in this situation?"

When you are exploring the truth, you don't squash your emotions or ignore your story; you do your best to set them aside. Imagine you are stepping across a bridge from the Story Chamber to the Truth Chamber and that the river you cross helps wash away your fears, attachment, and the drama of the situation.

Visualize the Truth Chamber as an expansive, light-filled space with large windows where you can see the Story Chamber from a place of witnessing.

State the facts as you see them. Imagine you are a scientist looking only at the hard physical evidence before you.

"What do I know is true in this situation?"

Again, the basic truth I always start with is: "I am breathing." When you can't find the truth, you can always come back to these three words: "I am breathing."

Even if this is the only truth you can grasp onto at the moment, you can keep going through the practice. "I am breathing." Okay. That is true. Even though you have all the feelings and all this story going on, just stay with "I am here, and I am breathing." And as you simply breathe, you might find that another level of the truth bubbles up from your inner wisdom. Remember, getting to the truth is a feeling; it is a knowing it in the body.

### Discovering Simplicity

Sometimes we fear the truth because we are afraid it will hurt worse than the story. And in the short run, that is *sometimes* true; the truth can feel like a sword that lances open an old wound. But the truth is always the medicine. Sometimes the medicine is bitter and difficult to swallow, but it is better than the slow, corrosive inner poison of a judgmental or victimizing story.

Now let's revisit my story around finances; there was good medicine to be found in the crisis. I realized that not checking my balance on a regular basis to see how we were doing as an organization was not a sustainable business practice. The truth was that I needed a bigger financial picture to predict the ebbs and flows and adjust accordingly. I had to acknowledge that I was responsible for the bottom line of the organization and that since financial planning is something I struggle with, I was going to need more help and more education. That was just the factual truth.

While my story wanted to keep hooking my attention, I chose to keep my focus on what was true, and with faith to take action. This did not make the problem go away. I still had to make some difficult choices. But with my feet firmly planted in the Truth Chamber, I could take the next steps from a place of clarity and self-respect, without being pummeled by my mind for being bad or wrong for my previous choices.

As Byron Katie writes, an unquestioned mind is a world of suffering. In the Truth Chamber, we are bravely questioning our mind. Don't let your mind tell you that questioning the story will create more suffering. It is lying. Remember, your Little Soul is desperately trying to stay in charge, and it will do anything to keep you hooked and living in the confines of the Story Chamber. Have compassion for your Little Soul, and keep turning your face toward the sunshine of your Big Soul and the clarifying light that streams through the Truth Chamber.

It's impossible to have one foot in the Story Chamber and one foot in the Truth Chamber. You must pick: Story or Truth. If you choose to hang out longer in the Story Chamber, don't judge yourself. Put both feet back in the Story Chamber and enjoy the story. Watch how your story creates suffering. Don't abandon yourself for your choice; use your time in the Story Chamber to learn about how your mind and emotions work. One day, when there is no judgment, you'll naturally find yourself yearning to know the truth. Or the truth will unexpectedly show up and wrap you in an embrace like an old welcome friend.

When we are spinning emotions and our story, or repressing

our emotions and pretending we don't have a story, or trying to make the story "nice" or "spiritual," we are putting our body and mind under tremendous stress. Most of our stories are based in fear and come from what I call *disaster mind.* Disaster mind is when your mind is hijacked by your lost Little Soul, who is frantically trying to manage the world.

Disaster mind is constantly looking at the worst-case scenario, seeing everything through the eyes of fear, worry, and anxiety. When we live this way, our heart rate increases, our breathing shallows, our adrenal glands get activated, and we are constantly on high alert for bad things to happen. Even if they are not happening in the moment, disaster mind makes them happen for us over and over again by visualizing what *might* happen or what *did* happen and how hard it was.

## Kirsten: Finding a New Balance

Moving through the last quarter of my apprenticeship with HeatherAsh, on a daily basis, I could see and feel shifts of awareness and the lightness of my soul. These shifts or openings occurred as I let go of stories, allowed buried emotions to surface, and held still enough for the insights and integration. One day, I was offered an amazing opportunity to practice the process of moving through each of the four chambers of the Warrior Heart.

I was at the local yoga studio, where I practiced regularly. As I breathed, flowed, and allowed myself to fully arrive on my mat, I began to feel a dizziness. This dizziness at first startled me and then immensely scared me. I continued with my mantras of

"I am . . . neutral, balanced, love, joy, open," only to feel more and more dizzy. I found myself falling out of poses that had never challenged me, feeling as if I had been drugged, feeling as if there were moments when I actually physically disappeared, then eventually slowing down enough to catch my breath and find balance again.

This dizziness continued to occur sporadically during my morning yoga practice. Each time I became dizzy, I witnessed and watched myself travel through each of the Warrior Heart chambers. I watched as I drifted through Intent, Feeling, Story, and Truth. I acknowledged my intent to be balanced, feel whole, full of joy and love, while also feeling scared, alone, and unsafe. I then heard the stories I created from this place of fear. "I am becoming physically unbalanced just like my mom. I will need outside help because I will no longer drive my car. I am losing control of my ability to take care of my body and live independently. I will no longer be safe to do things on my own." The stories spun out in all directions, in front of me, behind me, above and below me. I then witnessed myself slip into the Truth. The truth was that I was on my yoga mat right here and now. The truth was that I had and would continue to practice balance (unlike my mom). The truth was that I was safe in that beautiful room filled with loving and kind friends and that I always had the choice to rest in child's pose until my balance returned.

The truth was that I wasn't any of these stories that I had started to create. I then felt myself simultaneously move into my heart, into my feelings, into my intent, into the truth, and into the balance and neutrality of it all. I didn't have to play it safe by hiding from the edge or denying it existed. I only had to find the center of my Warrior Heart by releasing my tight grasp, letting go of old agreements, beliefs, and fears, while trusting in the balance and neutrality that were always within me. In the center of my Warrior Heart, I felt my world shift and adjust, and I fully trusted this new openness, emptiness, and fullness.

The Truth Chamber is where we learn to step beyond disaster mind and see through the eyes of our Big Soul. It's the difference between being the child having a temper tantrum and believing the world is over, and a well-rested loving parent who is watching the child have the tantrum, knowing it will be over soon.

Now, there are two different types of truth: relative truth and absolute truth. Relative truth is what we are experiencing in this moment. All our emotions and all our stories are true in the moment we are believing them. They are temporary constructs that are made real by our attention. This doesn't make them less painful or less beautiful. But they are not the absolute truth. When you say, "I am sad," you will not be sad every moment of every day for the rest of your life. When you say, "My heart is broken," after the end of a relationship, your heart will not always feel hurt. Everything changes. When we recognize relative truth, we hold our emotions and stories more lightly.

Absolute truth is more enduring. *The sky is blue. Water is fluid. My cousin is dying of cancer.*

But even what appears to be absolute truth can change: *The sky is orange at sunset. Water is solid when frozen. My cousin is now in remission.*

So to get to absolute truth, we must be clear and precise. *The sky is blue during the day. Water is fluid at room temperature. My cousin had cancer and is now in remission.*

All truths can shift and change depending on your perspective. If you believe something strongly, it is true for you. And yet, there may be a larger truth that will help you unhook from mental suffering and connect to more spaciousness and freedom.

As we work to discover the truth, let's look toward what we know to be true at the time—relative or absolute—*separate* from our own story.

Working in the truth room invites us to separate out anything that is a story and acknowledge and speak the difference between relative and absolute truth.

In regard to relative truth, it is helpful to change your language around the changeable truth of your emotions. Feel the difference between "I am sad" and "I am feeling sad" or "Sadness is present." One makes sadness who we are, and the other names sadness as something that will come and go like the clouds in the sky.

In the Truth Chamber, you step away from your story and your emotions enough to see them both with the eyes of love. The main hallmark of the Truth Chamber is the absence of judgment. Everything is just the way it is. Period. And this leads to a beautiful, enduring inner peace and stillness.

## Standing in Stillness

The Truth Chamber teaches you to stand in stillness. This means getting comfortable with not knowing and without needing to know: *What will happen next? But what if . . .* Your Little

Soul will yell in an effort to get your attention. Let the stillness of your Big Soul scoop up that scared child and hold your Little Soul tight.

A mother doesn't need to use a lot of words to comfort a small child. In this same way, you don't need to convince, explain, or debate with your Little Soul. Just hold it close. "I've got you. Rest into me."

As your Little Soul feels held and learns to trust your Big Soul again, you'll find that when your mind gets ruffled or scared, it will turn toward your Big Soul and the stillness of the Truth Chamber rather than retreating into the noisy Story Chamber.

In that still witness space, you'll be able to visit the Feeling and Story Chambers briefly to see what has become tangled and then move into the Truth Chamber to rest into the spacious simplicity of what you actually know to be true.

The more time you spend visiting the Truth Chamber and seeking the truth, the less time you'll want to spend unconsciously hanging out in the churn of the Story Chamber. Your habit of telling yourself stories will transform into a choice to tell yourself the truth.

The truth will diminish the strength and intensity of your story. The space that was filled by story then becomes available for your intuition, your creativity, and your inner peace to expand. Yes!

The difference between spending more time in the Truth Chamber and spending time in the Story Chamber is the difference between traveling on a newly paved freeway and a rough, potholed gravel road. Your life will become smoother. You'll be able to let go of the emotional dips of frustration, fear, and disappointment much more quickly. And you'll be able to start really enjoying the scenery that's all around you.

## Gina: The Gift of Time

*Gina recently wrote to me after she had a very upsetting experience that she was working to understand through the chambers:*

I'm so grateful for the perspective that time provides. It helps separate everything out. It's like what we were talking about with the Warrior Heart practice. To see the truth, sometimes all that is needed is time, and no pushing or wanting it to happen faster can change that. And then, all of a sudden, it's there . . . plain as day, and it was there all along. There is a deep truth here for me, and I will give it room to breathe and be revealed.

As you move through each of the chambers, remember that there are times when you will not be able to see the truth, or you will get stuck in your story, or you will be too frightened to sit with your emotions. Keep asking the questions. Open up space for insights and understanding. Don't demand the answers; invite them. Sometimes it may take hours, or even days, for the truth to present itself or for you to be able to witness rather than believe your story. Don't give up. Stay with the pace of your process.

Adding in our fourth Warrior Heart chamber, Intent, is like upgrading from an old, well-used car to a souped-up, fun convertible. Oh, the new places you will go when you start to embody the clarity of your Intent with the wisdom of your Truth! So now, let's step into the Intent Chamber and learn how one word can change everything.

## *Review*

### Truth Chamber Questions

- What is an ultimate truth right now?
- What is true about this situation?
- What do I wish were true versus what is actually a fact?
- How can I support myself in being with the truth?
- Is there any way that I am scared of seeing the truth?
- If I lived from the truth rather than my story, how would I experience the world differently?

The keys to opening the door of the Truth Chamber are creating a sense of spaciousness inside and the ability to listen to what is true.

When we connect to the truth, we move out of the pushing crowd of our stories and into a sanctuary of space and stillness. We no longer need to be right, or justify who we are, or understand. We want to know and embrace simplicity. We look toward the center of things, seeing through the tangles and walls of our thoughts. We allow the fire of truth to purify and burn away everything that stands in our way.

## Truth Chamber Practices

### *Your Truth Chamber*

Imagine your Truth Chamber as an actual space, just like you did with the Feeling and Story Chambers. What does your Truth Chamber look like? Make sure you consciously create your Truth Chamber so it reflects a feeling sense of spaciousness, openness, and ease. Is it inside or outside? What does the light look like in the space, and how big is it? Are there large glass windows with sunlight streaming in, or is it softly lit with candles? Is the floor carpeted with soft, squishy rugs or a cool, solid marble? Close your eyes and visualize your Truth Chamber, or write about it. You can also make a painting or a collage, or find a picture on the internet or in a magazine that best reflects your Truth Chamber.

### Journaling

Every morning, take three minutes to write out whatever truths you can see around you. What do you know is true, in this moment? "I am breathing. The wall is beige. My mother is sick with the flu. I feel agitated right now. The plant in the corner of my bedroom is a ficus." If you notice you start going into story (justifying or thinking about things), simply put a period at the end of the sentence and then look around for what else is true in this moment.

### Observer Glasses

Imagine you have a pair of glasses, and when you put them on, you are able to objectively observe the world around you. Your observer glasses filter out the drama of your story, to reveal only the truth that lies beneath. They also help you to see your emotions as real experiences that are temporary. With your observer glasses, you are able to witness your emotions, observe your story, and perceive what might have been clouded by them. Get really specific about what you see and what you sense. Instead of saying, "I feel hurt by his actions," say, "He was late the last three times we agreed to meet." What is actually true, separate from how you feel about it or what your story is? You are not using your observer glasses to discount the story or your emotions but simply to start to train yourself to separate out emotions, thoughts, and observations.

### The Third-Person Game

To help you create more spaciousness between yourself and your story so you can more easily connect to the truth, play the third-person game. Instead of saying, "I" when you talk about yourself (or to yourself), say your first name. So, for example, instead of saying, "I wish it wasn't so cold today," I would say, "HeatherAsh wishes it wasn't so cold today." Instead of saying, "I am annoyed," I would say, "HeatherAsh is annoyed." You can play this game in your own head, or with friends if they are also willing to play, or when you write in your journal. It helps break your personal identification with your story and your emotions and allows you to start being in tune with yourself from a totally different perspective.

# 6

# The Intent Chamber

*The self-confidence of the warrior is not the self-confidence of the average man. The average man seeks certainty in the eyes of the onlooker and calls this self-confidence. The warrior seeks impeccability in his own eyes and calls that humbleness. The average man is hooked to his fellow men, while the warrior is hooked only to infinity.*

—CARLOS CASTANEDA

ONE DAY, AFTER USING the Warrior Heart practice to find my center following a huge, in-my-face challenge, I thought, *Whoa, this really works!*

Here's the story.... A friend and I had spent two years talking and exploring the possibility of being in a romantic relationship. We decided to try something new, so instead of diving in headfirst, we got to know each other slowly. We text-messaged questions to each other and shared our wants and desires. Together we processed unfinished emotions from old relationships. Basically, we got to know each other from a distance (we lived in different states) and deepened our friendship and love whenever we could be together. We went to a lot of museums, went on many walks, and traveled together when we could.

We were both dating other people at the same time, and so we practiced being super honest about all our relationships and feelings. I felt like an adult learning how to communicate and be spacious in dating rather than do my usual behavior of going from zero to one hundred without really knowing the other person outside of the chemical attraction and fantasy.

One day, a series of events happened, and I decided, *Okay, I am in 100 percent. I'm ready to commit to this person and see what a relationship would look like.* Unbeknownst to me, he made a decision right around that time: *Okay, this is not going to work. I think there is something else better waiting for both of us.*

And so, as fate would have it, we both showed up for a week-long course I was teaching. I was excited to tell him what I'd realized, unaware that he had something else to share with me.

Before the class started, I told him, "Can we spend a week alone, just you and me, and really see what is here?" He dropped his gaze. And I felt my stomach plummet to my toes. Oh. The feeling I had earlier that he was going to be attracted to someone else was actually true. I waited.

"Well, there is something I need to share with you, and I'm scared to tell you."

"Go ahead," I said, knowing what was coming. (My intuitive sense is superstrong.)

"I'm attracted to someone here at the workshop."

He went on to tell me that he wanted to follow and explore his attraction to this other woman.

"If you choose to pursue her, it is completely over romantically between us," I heard myself say.

And then over the next week, I watched as he fell in love with someone else.

Now, this would be a difficult situation for anyone. It was compounded for me because many years ago, I watched my ex-husband fall in love with my main teaching partner. So to say that there is a little wound there is an understatement. While the situations were *not* the same, there was enough of a resonance that I was thrown into an old story and a lot of hurt.

There were days when I was teaching that I couldn't look at him, because I knew I would start crying. He was happily oblivious to my reaction; his eyes filled with his new love and the joy they were finding getting to know each other.

I tried my best to manage my emotions and stay professional. But at times, my pain leaked out despite my best effort to hold steady and honor his choice.

One day, we were all going on an excursion, and I asked if he wanted to go for a walk with me. "I already have plans," he said, looking with doe eyes at his new beloved. I felt crushed, and as I watched them walk away, the tears and overwhelm of emotions hit me like a tidal wave.

"Okay, time to go to your room," I said out loud to myself as I stood alone, uncertain about what to do next.

I found a place to sit, leaned against the wall, and closed my eyes.

"What are you feeling, Ash?"

*Disappointment. Sorrow. Abandoned.*

"And what is the story?"

*This always happens! The guy always picks someone else! And now it is going to be messy between us.*

"Truth?"

*He gets to choose. Oh! And I get to choose.*

"And what is your Intent for this situation?"

*Unconditional love. I want to love myself and others regardless of their choices.*
"And what do you want to choose now?"
*I want to go for a walk and enjoy this beautiful day.*

Now, there was much more processing to come around this situation, which stirred up a lot of old past stories and pain. But in that moment, I was free. Instead of spinning my emotions and story into an illusionary knot of bitterness, blame, or betrayal, I could stay with the truth: He gets to choose whom he wants to be in a relationship with. I get to choose my next step. And my focus was to learn how to engage out of love, for both myself and for him. And I could have a sweet walk with myself, enjoying my own company.

Truth and Intent are not concepts that have a lot of words to describe them. They are both a feeling in the body and an instinctual knowing that sings out like a church bell on a clear morning.

So if you find yourself using a lot of words to explain the truth, you are back in story rather than body feeling and instinct.

The same holds with the Intent Chamber, our fourth area of exploration, which requires very few words.

Intent is our focus, our will, and our warrior commitment to follow the pathway we choose.

Intent is not something we are wishing or hoping for; intent is something that we are willing to put our entire being behind, say a full-bodied *yes* to, and then take action to move *toward*.

When you enter the Intent Chamber, your query is: *What do I want?*

Ah, that short question, so simple but so powerful.

It is vital that the answer comes from your heart rather than from your head. Intent works best when it is directed from your loving compassion, rather than being pushed or forced by your judge or critical mind.

To get clear on your intent, it is important to tell yourself the truth about what you want for the specific situation you are bringing through the Warrior Heart practice. Pay attention to focusing on *your* intent and not about how you want the other person to act or be, or how you wish the situation were different. Watch how your mind may want to divert you back into wanting to change others rather than feeling into your intent.

The word *intent* encapsulates how you want to feel or what you want to bring to the situation you are working with.

As you work in the Intent Chamber, you don't want to drag your story into the upper chambers and muddy your intent with excess words and ideas. This is why I invite you to pick *one* word (yes, a hyphenated word is okay!) to represent your intent.

Whatever issue you are working through with the Warrior Heart practice, your intent comes from delving into the question: *What do I want?* For each different situation that you are in, you may have a different intent.

The Intent you choose will have a direct impact on what you do next, so pick your intent carefully. For example, if I'm struggling with a family member and I come to the Intent Chamber and get quiet, my Intent might be "compassion." I want to have more compassion for myself and my family member. Or my Intent might be "truth" because I realize that I need to express my truth. The differences between those two are radical in defining what action I take next. So if my intent is compassion, I'm going to act one way. If my intent is telling the truth no matter what, because I've been repressing speaking it, that's going to look a different way. Can you feel the difference?

Your intent is your North Star. It's your clear focus about where you are going. And it's going to dictate what you do next. Once you know the truth, or even if your truth is "I am breathing" and that's as far as you get, that's okay. Questions to ask when you step into the Intent Chamber are: *All right, sweetie, what's your intent? What do you want for yourself? What's the quality that you're working to bring into this moment or to practice?*

## Here Are Some Steps That Will Help You in Getting Clear on Your Intent:

1. Take your time.

   In the Truth Chamber, take your time bringing the feeling sense of the truth into your body. Don't try to rush through the Truth Chamber to get to the Intent Chamber. The more you can rest into your truth, the easier it will be to name your intent.

2. Imagine stepping into the Intent Chamber, another bright and airy space that is adjacent to the Truth Chamber.

   Visualize a beautiful, soothing, inspiring landscape or room that houses the unconditional love and awareness of unity of your Big Soul. I sometimes like to imagine that the Intent Chamber is where my wise highest self lives. When I step into this room, Big Soul holds my hands and looks me in the eye and reminds me, without words, that everything is going to be okay, and that I am powerful beyond measure.

3. Imagine you can look at the entire situation as a witness. How is the story you have been telling yourself connected to your own inner work? How can it be in service to you?

Stand with your Big Soul (or your higher self) and imagine flying high above the drama, fear, and scarcity of your story. What do you see? How is this experience you are having now perfect for helping you to clean and clear your old beliefs and agreements so that you can come back into connection with your Big Soul?

4. Breathe and imagine that you can empty yourself. Be a vessel waiting to be filled. Invite your Intent to arise from your deepest heart space.

Let everything else go, all thoughts and beliefs, and simply sit in silence for a while. Breathe in presence, breathe out distraction. Breathe in peace, breathe out worry. Breathe in emptiness, breathe out busyness. Rest into the stillness within yourself without expectation or striving.

As you explore the Intent Chamber, it is helpful to use the Eagle method of what we call *stalking* (more on the important process of stalking yourself in chapter 8). Eagles fly high above their prey, looking at the big picture of the land and waiting until they see movement before they swoop down. Spending time in the Truth Chamber, like the eagle flying high above its prey, will help you to get a bit of distance from your emotions and story.

Now in the Intent Chamber, step back even further and explore the story in relation to what you are working on now in your life. How can this situation be a way to help you grow, deepen, or heal? How is it asking you to stretch and respond in a new way? How are you being challenged to change and come to a new choice?

## Li: A New Relationship with My Body

*My friend Li wrote to me about his experience using intent to help heal his body:*

One day while I was walking, I felt a sharp pain in my left knee. My mind immediately went into full alarm mode: I had torn something, or my body was aging and I was not going to be able to play the sports I enjoyed so much. I thought about my own father, who had several knee operations and at the end of his life could barely walk. He was in constant pain. As my mind spun more and more stories, I found that my knee was hurting worse than ever.

Then I heard your voice in my head, reminding me of how powerful my mind was. I found a café and pulled out my journal and starting doing the Warrior Heart practice.

When I got to the Intent Chamber, I wondered what my new focus would be. After several minutes, I realized it was "Presence." My story was trying to connect me to my father and to his struggles. Instead, I wanted to stay in dialogue with my body and what it needed.

With my intent now firmly connected to staying present, I put my journal back in my backpack and started walking again. Every time my mind wanted to jump to a story about the pain I was experiencing, I took a breath and brought my attention back to the actual physical sensation in my knee. I noticed that if I shifted my weight slightly to the inside of my foot, the pain went away. As I kept opening to new possibilities, I had an insight that maybe I simply needed new shoes. I later made an appointment with a podiatrist, who confirmed my intuition and taught me what kind of support my foot needed to keep my knees stable.

That intent has continued to bring gifts into my life. Now whenever I notice myself getting sick or there is pain in my body, I immediately come back into the present and ask my intuition and inner guidance what my body needs to be at its optimum. This has totally changed my relationship with my own body. I'm so grateful!

It is so beautiful when we can stay in our heart and ask questions that will help us unravel past stories and agreements. Again, the right questions and the Warrior Heart practice don't make those hard life situations go away. But they do completely change our relationship with our challenges and help us choose a road forward rather than feeling like we are being dragged along behind a car.

Going back to my story, after I set my intent to hold unconditional love and continued on my walk, I kept opening to what the bigger picture was. As I strolled along, I felt my old stories fall apart and crumble like a house created out of mud bricks. I understood in my bones that to love unconditionally means to let go. While I could still feel a sense of disappointment in my belly, I honored myself and my desires and just let the disappointment be there. Disappointment was present, and I could unconditionally love the disappointment as well.

And then I had a realization that made me stop and laugh for a long time.

There was a part of my Little Soul that felt she was getting punished. I mean, really, having someone I was wanting to partner with fall in love with someone else right in front of me? Again? What kind of a cruel joke was this? But instead of following that old, worn-out, and depressing story, I kept going back to my Intent and the Truth. Each step, I thought, *Unconditional love. I get to choose. Unconditional love. I get to choose. Unconditional love. He gets to choose. Unconditional love. I get to choose.*

And then another realization struck. *The universe loves me so much that it is giving me a frigging Ph.D. in letting go!*

I was not being punished by this situation. I was being shown how to release someone gracefully, rather than clinging stubbornly like I had done with my ex-husband. I was getting another opportunity to practice unconditional love. It sucked, but it was also perfect. Would I choose to love myself this time and let go with a blessing, or grasp tighter with both hands and try to control the situation?

I let go.

Believe me, it was not easy. There were several more really intense conversations with this man and a few more trips for me through the four chambers. But once I saw that I had an opportunity to practice my intent of unconditional love, I felt a fire reignite in my belly, and I felt the support of the universe. I knew where to keep redirecting my attention. I knew I could do this, knowing it would be less messy this time and a bit more graceful.

I kept reminding myself that I didn't have to be perfect; I just had to stay with myself through the practice, be honest, and keep looking toward the clear light of my truth and intent.

Your intent is not something you're going to master right away. Your intent is where you are willing to practice and learn and grow.

Keep asking yourself, *What is my intent in this current situation I'm working with?*

And like the Truth Chamber, your Intent is not a story but

more of a spacious knowing that you are willing to commit to. Let's look deeper into what intent is and is not.

## *What Is Intent?*

First, let's look at what intent is not. It is not wishing or hoping for something or demanding or forcing things to happen. It is your full-bodied commitment to an action or an ideal and your willingness to stay with it, over time, as long as it takes.

When I set my intent, I get really present and bring my awareness into the center of my chest and solar plexus. I bring the feeling sense of the quality I want to commit to and plant that seed in my heart. Then I align my will, or warrior focus, with that seed of intent. I then open myself energetically, to align with Life so that I may connect with the larger Intent that moves through all things.

Then I name a few different intents out loud to see which one resonates with me the most.

My intent is to love unconditionally.
My intent is to trust.
My intent is to have compassion.

I hold the situation I am working with in my mind and ask my Big Soul wise self to help me pick the best intent to help me free myself from my story. Once I've picked my intent, I repeat it out loud three times:

My intent is to love unconditionally.
My intent is to love unconditionally.
My intent is to love unconditionally.

And then I let it go.

When we choose an intent, we commit to it *and* release it completely.

Setting intent in this way is a form of prayer. Not the type of prayer where you are in crisis and you are suddenly begging or demanding God to help you. Intent prayer is a type of prayer where you are living in faith and communion with the Divine.

My favorite story about this type of prayer is a man asking a nun what time of day she prays. She responds that she doesn't pray at a specific time. He is confused and says, "But you are a nun. I thought you prayed at specific times!" She answers, "You don't understand. My entire life is my prayer."

The key behind connecting your intent to the larger picture is this: to listen and have gratitude. Embody the wisdom of Meister Eckhart: "If the only prayer you ever say in your entire life is thank you, it will be enough."

It takes time to cultivate this type of a prayerful relationship with your personal intent aligning with Universal Intent.

Imagine a small stream merging with a larger stream and how much more powerful the two streams are together. This is the energy of personal intent aligning with Universal Intent, or the Little Soul aligning with the Big Soul.

Intent is the larger flow of the universe; Life dreaming itself into form. Our Big Soul is intimately connected to the universe of possibility and magic. Whether you call this force *God, Allah, Divine, Creator, Higher Self, Goddess, Love,* or any other name, this invisible web not only unites the hearts and souls of all humans together but also connects us to the plants, animals, rocks, and sky.

Your essence's Intent is for expansion and expression. Again, your Big Soul is like a wise elder who loves you unconditionally and is excited to see you grow into the best possible version of yourself.

Intent is a force that we harness rather than something that we demand. This is the key to understanding Intent.

It's the difference between using your will to control or fix, or using your will aligned with a larger force, which means the willingness to surrender your desires to the highest good.

It's the difference between living from the needs and fears of your Little Soul and living connected to the wisdom and clarity of your Big Soul.

Remember that your Little Soul's desire is for safety and familiarity. Your Little Soul is like a hoarder that wants to hold on to everything, even the things you've outgrown.

Your Little Soul wants to control, fix, force.

Your Big Soul waits, listens, and then consciously connects with the larger river of Intent.

For now, we want to learn how to leave the Little Soul behind in the Story Chamber and connect to our Big Soul in the Truth and Intent Chambers. *Warning!* It is so important that you do not get caught up in believing that living in the Intent and Truth Chambers is "superior" to the Story or Feeling Chambers. This will lead to the temptation to disown your story, to make it "bad" or "wrong," and/or to spiritually bypass your emotions. All the chambers are equal, and all are important. Your story makes up who you are. Becoming intimate with your story and your emotions is a beautiful part of being human. It will also make you less judgmental toward yourself and other people.

How do you know if you are setting intent from your Little Soul or your Big Soul?

Your Little Soul will focus on what the "other" needs to do or how the situation should be different. Basically, your Little

Soul operates on conditional love, which translates to "I'll love if . . ." And its relationship with intent is the same: "I'll change/grow/surrender if . . ."

Here are some examples of setting conditional intent:

**Forgiveness:** *I'll forgive them only if they apologize first.*

**Love:** *I'll love if they show love first.*

**Compassion:** *I'll have compassion only when they change their behavior.*

**Surrender:** *I'll let go of the situation only when I understand it.*

Setting your intent is the radical choice of committing to a new action no matter what.

**Forgiveness:** *I will forgive even if they don't apologize.*

**Love:** *I will love even if they don't love me back.*

**Compassion:** *I will have compassion for their behavior even if I don't agree with it.*

**Surrender:** *I will surrender even if I don't understand.*

Here are some examples of words you can use for your intent:

creativity
confidence
clarity
wisdom
freedom

compassion
love
peace
healing
steady
grounded
present
happy
openhearted
patient

Having a clear intent and taking new action do not mean that you will always agree with or condone others' behavior or choices. It doesn't mean that you never set boundaries or that you stay in situations that are not serving you. It means that you are willing to claim your own freedom to choose how you want to feel and how you want to consciously navigate the situation as you move forward.

Your intent is your sacred bond to yourself to practice responding in a new way.

## The Wisdom of Not Knowing

When we live in the Story Chamber, our Little Soul is in charge, and its entire focus is on understanding, isolation, and control. But when we begin to work with Intent, we are reconnecting with our Big Soul, whose domains are possibility, connection, and mystery.

In order for you to stop Little Soul from grabbing your intent and trying to sabotage it, you must let it go.

If you try to control, direct, or even understand how to manifest your intent, your Little Soul will come in with judgment or victimization. It will either judge you for not manifesting your intent "properly" or it will feel overwhelmed and freaked out that things are not going "right."

Instead, keep surrendering up how it is supposed to happen. The path of the warrior is 100 percent commitment combined with 100 percent faith. Don't allow your actions to come from worry or fear (Little Soul). Let them come from your intuition and knowing (Big Soul).

How do you stay in the most effective relationship with your intent? The key is not to think about your intent but to feel it in your bones. Keep moving from how you want a situation to turn out to how you want to feel in the situation.

Knowing your intent doesn't mean you're going to be able to change other people. You don't have that power. People might change as you move forward with a new intent, but that can't be your focus. Your focus has to be on how you are going to change and allowing other people to be who they are. A Warrior of the Heart does not caretake or try to fix others. A Warrior of the Heart respects other people's decisions and choices and knows that each individual is the keeper of their own intent.

## Pauline: Ending a Pattern in Relationships

Several years ago, I went through a difficult divorce. I hadn't realized how emotionally abusive my relationship was until I finally ended it. I spent a couple of years healing and learning about what old family agreements I was carrying that caused me to stay in such a challenging and unhealthy relationship. Through reading HeatherAsh's books and going to workshops, I slowly learned how to stop caretaking others and to begin letting go of a very old belief that I was only safe if I was being nice and agreeable to everyone.

When I first started dating, I wasn't totally clear what I wanted. My focus was completely on who I wanted them not to be. (Not narcissistic, not verbally abusive, not in another relationship.) Every time I dated someone who showed a tiny bit of kindness or maturity, I'd think, *This must be it!!!* without really knowing anything about them. I would try to get them to commit quickly, which backfired. I started to hate dating, feeling that the "good" women were already taken.

When we did the Warrior Heart practice in Sedona, I finally understood that I was dating in reaction to my story, rather than being clear with what I actually wanted. When I talked to another woman at the workshop about intent and what we wanted, I discovered that my focus at this time of my life was a desire for adventure, not the comfort I had always sought. Wow! That has changed everything! Now dating is not something "separate" from the rest of my life; it is another opportunity for adventure. Every date I go on, I am curious to see what kind of adventure we can create together. I'm not trying to force anything to happen or to be anyone at all. I'm learning. Sometimes I realize quickly we are very different, and I don't try to force things to happen. I find I'm more playful and excited just to explore and see what the next adventure is. There is no pressure or expectation. And I know one day I'll find someone who is the best adventure partner for me.

Because you can't control other people, how situations unfold is not 100 percent up to you . . . there are always variables. What you can control, through your intent, is the decisions you make and how you will respond.

Just like truth is a higher octave of your story, your intent is a higher octave of feeling. Intent is a feeling consciously directed.

Live your intent as a prayer. Keep asking the Divine/Creator/God/Life to guide you forward in the best way to manifest your intent. Listen for guidance. Take action. Learn as you go along. Repeat.

Living in the mystery allows miracles to arise. When you think you know how things should be, you collapse possibilities into one singular point.

Living in the mystery can be uncomfortable, especially at first. Not knowing how your intent is going to manifest can be uncomfortable. Letting go of needing to know the exact *how* and *why* can be uncomfortable. And breaking old patterns of behavior is often very uncomfortable.

Getting comfortable with discomfort, ambiguity, not knowing, and the mystery is crucial *if* you are going to step beyond the fixed perception of your Little Soul to connect with the wavelike, creative, expanded state of your Big Soul. You will need to let your Little Soul be uncomfortable to do this. Keep soothing your Little Soul with sweet words and encouragement, but don't allow it to drag you back to trying to understand and fixate on how things should be. Keep letting go. Keep trusting. Keep going back to your intent, over and over again.

## And Then There Is This ... On Petty Tyrants

As a Warrior of the Heart, the person about whom you think, *If they just disappeared forever or changed completely, I'd finally be happy,* is going to be your biggest teacher. Praise for the people we call *petty tyrants.*

A petty tyrant is that one person who can make your life miserable with one word or a glance. Petty tyrants are overbearing; mean; judgmental; never satisfied; filled with sparking, barely controlled rage; or calculating in their cruelness. It often feels like the person you consider your petty tyrant is out to get you, and no matter what you do, they are winning a game you don't want to be playing.

To a normal human, a petty tyrant is someone to be avoided at all costs. They are seen as an isolated problem that needs to be removed so we can get on with enjoying our lives.

And yet, have you noticed how often when one petty tyrant leaves, another seems to take their place like a weed with very deep roots? And indeed, the roots of the petty tyrant are deep, and they will keep sprouting in your work or home until you claim your Warrior Heart and turn and face yourself.

For the roots of all discord from a petty tyrant lie not within them but within us.

A petty tyrant is the ultimate challenge for a Warrior of the Heart, a worthy adversary that will stretch you to hold on to and manifest your intent not in spite of who they are but because of who they will help you become. But only if you turn and face the challenge.

Let me back up a bit and share a story with you that will make the concept of a petty tyrant clearer.

Nature brings us so many lessons. This lesson is about trees, and wind.

In the early '70s in Arizona, a team of scientists created a biosphere: an entirely sealed environment where people lived for three years. Everything to sustain life was included, including gardens and trees.

For three years, the trees grew at astonishing rates.

And then one day, all the trees fell over.

When the scientists opened up the biosphere and studied what happened, they learned something incredible: Trees need wind to find their strength and stability.

Your personal petty tyrant is your wind.

Now, remember: You don't have to go out looking for the wind. Or for a petty tyrant. They will come to you. So often, a petty tyrant is your boss, or an ex-lover, or a parent. A petty tyrant is the person who triggers you the most, who pushes all your buttons, who can reduce you in seconds flat from a calm, rational adult to a scared, little, overwhelmed child or a snarling, cornered animal, fangs and claws sharp.

And believe me, they are going to be the crème of the crème for helping you to hold on and live your intent.

A petty tyrant is going to mirror to you, where no one else can, where exactly you are still holding on to old stories and struggles. Don't be swayed thinking it is the petty tyrant that needs to change. Instead, use the petty tyrants in your life to commit more strongly to your intent and to help you develop an unbreakable strength at your core.

Here is how to work a petty tyrant through the chambers and how to activate the power of your intent to transform your relationship with them:

**Feeling Chamber:** How do they make you feel about yourself? Sit in the feelings without running the story about why you feel the way you do. Just feel the unfiltered emotions. Look for and explore the sensations of any shame, blame, despair, and/or rage.

**Story Chamber:** How do you think the petty tyrant should be different? How do you wish you were different? Are you blaming yourself or blaming them? What is the older story line that is being resonated in the present by your petty tyrant?

**Truth Chamber:** Say to yourself, *I am not going to be able to change my petty tyrant. I choose to change myself.* Now look at what is true in your current interaction.

**Intent Chamber:** What do you want for *yourself* in relation to your petty tyrant? (Again, it is crucial to remember that the Intent Chamber is not about your intent for how you want the other person to be!)

I've had several spectacular petty tyrants who in the beginning I felt were ruining my life. But once I learned how to harness the power of my Warrior Heart and use the four chambers to go deeper, I found that every single petty tyrant was a blessing in disguise. Working with a petty tyrant does not mean you must stay in situations that are unhealthy for you or that you never make boundaries. Sometimes the very lesson of a petty tyrant is to teach you how to say no or when to walk away. Sometimes the lesson is to recognize that you are your own petty tyrant; the other person is just acting as a helpful mirror. Sometimes the lesson is to recover the power you have given away to the other person. And sometimes the lesson is in how you learn to stretch yourself past where you thought you could go to learn how to hold your intent in relation with your petty tyrant. Do not expect your work unraveling your reactions to a petty tyrant to be easy or quick. But there are life-transforming, core-strengthening, mind-bending truths to be discovered beyond the stories and reactions.

In the next chapter, we will explore how to now take your intent back through the chambers. Your intent is your most powerful Warrior Heart tool for dismantling and freeing you from your old, heavy stories. Naming your intent is not the last step in the Warrior Heart practice but the beginning of a new way of being.

## *Review*

### Intent Chamber Questions

- What do I actually want in this situation?
- Where do I want to put my focus?
- What is my bigger focus in life right now, and how does this situation fit in?
- What word best describes where I want to put my attention?
- If I could experience anything in this situation, what would it be?
- If I could gift the world with one thing, what would it be?

The keys to opening the Intent Chamber are in taking total

responsibility for our lives and our choices and claiming both our personal accountability and direction.

Intent comes when we stop blaming others or shaming ourselves, and when we are dedicated to living in the truth and focusing on a new way of being. Self-responsibility is not about punishing ourselves into being better people but knowing where we want to practice taking action from. We understand that all our actions dictate our reality, and we use a specific word/intent to navigate our own inner ship.

## Intent Chamber Practices

### Your Intent Chamber

Imagine your Intent Chamber as an actual space, just Like you did with the three previous chambers. What does your Intent Chamber look like? Just like with your Truth Chamber, make sure you consciously create your Intent Chamber so it reflects a feeling sense of spaciousness, openness, and ease. How big is it? Is the space a clearing in the forest or a temple you once saw on television? What colors and artwork are in your Intent Chamber? What does it smell like? Close your eyes and visualize your Intent Chamber, or write about it. You can also make a painting or a collage, or find a picture on the internet or in a magazine that best reflects your Intent Chamber.

### Journaling

Every morning, take a moment to write out what your intent is for your day. Where do you want to put your focus today? Your intent might come from a recent Warrior Heart practice or might be based on whatever projects or tasks you need to do today. Whatever your intent is, write it in big letters in your journal, along with the date. Then the next day, go back over the previous day and write for three minutes about how you brought your intent into your day, or the places you struggled to hold your intent. Look especially for any insights about how you could better support yourself in living from your intent each day.

### Not Doings

One of my favorite ways to work with intent is to do what we call *not doings.* Here is the definition from my book *Warrior Goddess Training:* A *not doing* is an action that you take for no reason except to break old patterns. Some basic examples of not doings are eating with your nondominant hand, driving to work a different way each day, or digging a deep hole and then filling it up again. The goal of not doings is twofold: to help you learn to put 100 percent of yourself into an action for no reward or reason, and to shake up habitual ways of being.

To use not doings to strengthen your intent, ask yourself, *What unusual, unpredictable action can I take that will help me to embody my intent more fully?* You want to find an action that your mind basically says, *Why would we do this? It makes no sense!* If it makes sense or is logical, it is *not* a not doing; it is simply an action.

From a doctor who has realized she has become highly judgmental of others: "I'm going to water each of my plants for the next month using my grandmother's teacup while I bring all of my compassion to every sip I give them."

From a CEO of a company who is wanting to be more fluid: "I will get to work early and pull everything out of my desk drawers, clean everything thoroughly while I listen to opera, and then put everything back in a different drawer."

From a newly separated mother who wants to feel stronger as she navigates her divorce: "My not doing is to work out at a gym across town three days a week as a metaphor for building my inner strength."

Create a not doing where you can practice bringing 100 percent of your intent to what you are doing, without there being a logical reason or an obvious reward.

### Intent Meditation Practice

To deepen your relationship with your intent, use this simple but powerful intent meditation technique. Set a timer for one minute, which you will reset five times, for a total of five minutes (or set a meditation timer, such as Insight Timer, for five minutes with a reminder bell every minute). Start by saying your intent out loud three times. Then close your eyes and ask yourself where you experience feeling your intent in your body. (You might feel love in your heart, clarity in your temples, or courage in your belly, for example.) Breathe into the area you sense that you experience your intent.

Once the first bell goes off, bring your attention to fully experiencing your intent as a feeling state. Bring your intent from a thought to a sensation. So instead of thinking about compassion or faith, you are finding and experiencing the feeling of compassion or faith in your body. Use each one-minute interval to reconnect to the feeling sense of your intent. As you get more familiar with how to keep yourself connected and experiencing your intent, you can increase the time.

# 7

# Integration

*Ego says, "Once everything falls into place, I'll feel peace." Spirit says, "Find your peace, and then everything will fall into place."*

—MARIANNE WILLIAMSON

LAST SUMMER, I HAD the blessing of living in my new Airstream travel trailer in Woodstock, New York. My intent was to use the time to work on this book, be in nature, and hang out with my author friends.

There were major challenges from the beginning. The first campground where I stayed didn't have electricity. I had a solar panel, but it rained nonstop, and no sun means no power. My batteries ran out quickly, and four days into my adventure, I found myself without electricity. Later, I had the opportunity to deal with backing my brand-new trailer into a tree (yay, first dent!), driving all night to a campground, and then being too exhausted to navigate the Airstream into a tiny camp spot (thank you, kind neighbors, for helping!). I had a massive adventure driving onto Manhattan Island by mistake and then not being able to find a way off that was permissible for a truck and trailer (thank you, kind police officers, who sent me to yet another bridge/tunnel I wasn't allowed to cross!).

So as you can see, living in a twenty-foot house on wheels came with a very steep learning curve for me.

My last night in Woodstock was definitely some sort of Warrior Heart test.

Here is a part of my journal entry from that day:

Travel Date, Day 52; Star Date, September 2, 2018

How do you know when something is a warning versus an obstacle to overcome? This was my pondering at midnight a few nights ago as I switched out the hitch on my truck.

All week, I had been in a not-so-unfamiliar Libra spin: a choice between two things and not knowing which one to pick. In this case, the choice was between moving my Airstream and all of my belongings to Santa Fe, New Mexico (the original plan), or staying in Woodstock, New York (where I had spent the summer). During my time living in my Airstream in different areas of the Catskills, I'd fallen more deeply in love with Woodstock's trees, mountains, creeks, and people.

Should I stay or should I go?

So I prayed, and dreamed on it, and talked to friends, which didn't bring much more clarity. I made the agreement with myself that I would listen to my intuition and be open to any messages and that I could decide to stay or go at any time.

Departure date: Friday, August 31. On the evening of Thursday, August 30, I misplaced my truck key. Two hours of searching did not reveal its whereabouts, and so I went to bed, figuring I'd find it in the morning. When I woke up, I remembered I had a spare key in my suitcase that someone had made for me.

And then the friend, who was helping me pack, called to let me know his car kept breaking down. I headed to my truck to go pick him up, only to find my truck wouldn't start. *What?!?!*

After another couple of hours trying to get the truck started, the tow truck arrived. The driver immediately asked me, "Do you have the original key? It has a chip in it, and this may be why your truck is not starting."

"But I've used this key before!" I responded. But just to make sure, while my truck was towed to the Toyota dealer in the next town, my friend (whose car was now miraculously working) and I went to my storage unit to get the "real" extra key.

And ta-da, it worked!

But the story wasn't over. More obstacles to come.

We packed up my truck and tarped the load, and I hugged my friend goodbye.

And that is when I discovered that the motor that raises and lowers my hitch was not working. With a little sleuthing, I realized that when my friend and I had swapped out my bad batteries, we had hooked up the motor to the negative instead of the positive terminal. Easy fix. Onward.

But no. One more obstacle presented itself, with a smile, to me.

When I lowered the trailer onto the hitch, the added weight in the truck (twelve boxes of books and various altar boxes) caused the bottom of my huge, heavy-duty hitch to literally hit the ground.

Really?

At this point, I stopped everything and took a deep breath.

Was I not supposed to be leaving?

Were all these issues the universe's way of telling me to leave the Airstream in Woodstock and fly to Santa Fe for my workshop?

Here I was, all packed and ready to go, but I wasn't willing to force something that apparently wasn't supposed to happen.

If I was going to go, I would obviously need a new hitch.

"Okay, Spirit. If you do not want me to drive the Airstream to New Mexico, you need to give me one more sign. Otherwise, I'm going to buy a new hitch and see if that works."

I drove to a U-Haul dealer, bought two different types of hitches just to be on the safe side, then went to a movie, and then had tea with friends.

So, there I was, switching out my hitch after leaving their house at midnight. And *yes,* it worked!!!!

Two days into my journey, I had to giggle at all of the delays. But the beauty was that each delay invited me to get quiet, listen, clear out any emotion, and then move forward without forcing.

Throughout that day, I kept coming back to my intent: listen. I didn't expect things to go easily or not easily, or for people to help me make a decision or make things work. I stayed present with everything that was arising, stopped to listen, and stayed curious. Even though it was a totally crazy day, I remained happy and calm (with a few moments of panic). When I left New York, I was excited about what next new adventure was ahead of me.

I know that my ability to be resilient, flexible, and openhearted came from my work with the Warrior Heart practice and my dedication to living from my Intent and Truth and bringing them into the Story and Feeling Chambers over and over again.

But for many years, I had it backward. I believed that if I could only get my story straight, if I would just stop feeling these annoying emotions, or if only other people would change, I would feel better.

This is what many of us do. We put our focus outside of ourselves and expect or hope or demand that the world fit our needs.

As a Warrior of the Heart, you are now taking full responsibility for transforming your world from the inside out. The pivot point is when you are clear with your Intent and then turn around and go back through the chambers from last to first: Intent, Truth, Story, ending in the Feeling Chamber.

Why go backward through the chambers once you know your Intent?

The real power of the Warrior Heart practice begins at the end. You've traveled through your Feeling, Story, and Truth Chambers to the Intent Chamber. Now it is time to integrate your Intent and Truth into your life and create a more expansive, creative, and healing view of your story.

The only way to do this is by revisiting your Story through the eyes of your Intent and the Truth in your belly.

Here is one of the best ways I've found to use Intent combined with the Truth to help you unravel, clarify, and heal your Story.

## *Intent and Truth Holding Hands*

Imagine your Intent is not just a word, not just a quality, but an actual guide and mentor. Your Intent aligned with the universe will be your greatest ally, teacher, and butt kicker.

And believe me, you will be challenged as you integrate your Intent. You are going to be asked to stretch, grow, let go, open, and rewire your entire way of being in the world as you learn to live from your Intent. It will be beautiful, challenging, and the biggest gift you ever give to yourself.

In Ruth Gendler's brilliant book *The Book of Qualities,* she poetically personifies different emotions and states of being.

> "Courage has roots. She sleeps on a futon on the floor and lives close to the earth." "Fear has a long shadow, but he himself is quite small. He has a vivid imagination." "Pleasure is wild and sweet. She likes purple flowers." "Integrity takes long, thoughtful walks. When she comes home her pockets are filled with stones and shells and feathers."

So imagine that you are holding hands with the personification of your Intent. What would compassion, faith, or presence look and feel like? What would your Intent wear? Take your time writing a poem, or, with a few words, describe your Intent as a living, breathing, beneficial force.

Now imagine that your Intent grabs your hand and says, "Let's go, dear one!"

Together, you step into the Truth Chamber with your Intent. Pause here and look around the Truth Chamber. Ask your

Intent to help you see anything you may have missed before. What other truths are waiting for you to discover?

This is a good time to get quiet and spend a few minutes sitting silently, going for a walk, or doing any other integrating and nourishing activity. We need to pause and allow the wisdom of our Intent and Truth to permeate like rainwater into the soil of being. Rest into the Truth. Breathe into your Intent. Settle into the silence between the words.

As you spend more time in the Intent and Truth Chambers, you'll grow your ability to stay in this wordless, expansive place. Insights and understanding will percolate up from the core of your being, blossoming like flowers.

In this place of openness, you may find the story that you started out with will begin dissolving and you'll feel free. You'll recognize that the story has no more power over you, and you'll watch it come apart like yarn pulled from an old sweater that is coming unraveled.

Don't try to put the story back together again; just be with the Truth. Ask your Intent to guide you, to see if there is any cleanup or next steps to take.

Know that even if you feel completely detached from your story, you want to stay in the mystery and be open that it might tighten its net around you again and drag you back into the Story Chamber at some point in the future. That's okay. Any amount of spaciousness away from the story is informing your being about what is possible. Rest into that stillness for as long as you can. And when you feel the story pulling at you, be curious about where it is hooking you instead of fighting it.

You will not move back into living completely enmeshed in your Story Chamber; no. You are reentering the Story Chamber so that you can get to know the story line more intimately and see what your work is, to embody your Intent and Truth.

As you work the Warrior Heart practice, stay curious and open to whatever may arise in your Feeling or Story Chambers. Don't assume you know what you are Feeling, or that it is the same old Story as before, or that you know the Truth even before you've stepped into the Feeling, Story, or Truth Chambers. Be aware of the Little Soul's desire to keep blurring the lines between the chambers so it can trick you into thinking your Story is Truth and your Feeling is your Intent.

Keep the boundaries between the chambers clear, and systematically step into each chamber: Feeling, Story, Truth, Intent. Then go back to the Truth Chamber, revisit the Truth, and imagine you are now going to open the door to the Story Chamber with your awareness intact. Can you greet your story as an old friend?

While sometimes simply stating the truth and naming your intent are enough to release the story's hold on you, more often the story will still feel monstrous and all-consuming when you peek at it from the Truth Chamber (especially in the beginning when doing this work, or when it is a big issue).

This is where the real healing happens—in this warrior act of facing your story once again.

## Revisiting Your Story

When you are in the Truth and Intent Chambers, you are in the present moment. And when you are in the present moment, everything is fine. Life can be taken one step at a time. You are not freaking out about the past or disaster-minding the future.

Right here and right now, you are okay. That is the truth. And the other truth is that your work is just beginning, because now it is time to go back to the past.

Courageously step back into the Story Chamber.

You may feel completely assaulted by your story, or you may be able to easily witness it from a distance. There is no right or wrong about what it will be like when you go back into the Story Chamber; it will only be about where you are in relation to your story. Keep telling yourself the truth.

"Wow, I'm still really hooked by this story."

"Hmm, I can see how I can change the perspective of this story."

"Oh, this is a much older story than what I thought I was working with."

How are you perceiving your story now? Be honest. Don't dodge it or try to make it "better" or "worse." Hang out in the Story Chamber and see how your Intent and Truth can help you with what your next action is. Don't try to rush to find an action or an answer; sit in the discomfort. Call in all your warrior qualities. Wait. Listen. Explore.

Again, sometimes the process of releasing the story happens almost instantaneously once you know the truth and your intent. But other times, it can take days or even weeks to find a new way to be with your story.

Since your stories are often multilayered and rooted in much older and younger situations, you may have to explore your past to see what story lies beneath.

Here is an example of working through layers of the story from my own process so that you can see how it works.

Remember my story about witnessing my friend falling in love with another woman? When I went back into the Feeling Chamber, while I had more clarity around my story, I still felt the sinking stomach sensation of disappointment churning within me. As I let myself experience the emotion, I recognized that it was a familiar feeling. I took note and moved on with my day.

The sense of disappointment stayed with me for a couple of days, but now I was aware that it was not just about the current situation I was in. I felt the sensation of a younger version of myself being disappointed.

A very old story line was at play. Because I was able to stay curious about what other story was getting triggered by the disappointment I was feeling, I was able to see how my Little Soul / little-girl self was still holding on to an old story about needing her daddy to like her. Being rejected by my male friend was resonating with feeling unseen by my father for the times I felt he didn't accept me as a child.

Now, I have to say that it is somewhat easier to feel abandoned and rejected and upset about a current situation, because you have the evidence right in front of you. "Look, he did this, and it hurt me! He is making me feel this way!" It is humbling to realize that much older wounds are being touched that have nothing to do with someone else's action. And the truth is that this is the case more often than not. The beauty of awareness is that when you have the courage to put your attention where it needs to be—on the originating wound—the roots of your personal pain get exposed, and then you can bring it into the light and it can be healed. *What does this old story need to heal?* I asked myself. I went back into the Feeling Chamber to feel the pain of my younger self striving to be loved by her father. I visited the Story Chamber and saw how much I based my happiness on whether men I cared about liked or approved of me or not. I saw the truth: My value is not based on other people's opinions or choices. And I claimed my intent: self-acceptance.

Revisiting the Story Chamber allowed me to see how my adult self had grown tremendously, but my little-girl self still felt she had to prove herself to be loved. *What do you need?* I asked my little one.

And then I listened. And it was in holding all the parts of the process, my intent, my truth, my story, and my feelings, that I was able to see the perfection of being offered another opportunity to either accept or reject myself. My Ph.D. in letting go was really a Ph.D. in choosing to lovingly hold on to myself.

There is no time frame, no "right" way to work with your story. This is where your creativity, patience, and perseverance come in. With your Intent and the Truth as your guides, you'll be able to listen for the next step in your evolution and healing.

Keep going back to the Intent and Truth Chambers often. Give yourself all the time you need to work out the pain and feeling that is trapped in your story. I like to remind myself, *I'm in for the long haul with you, HeatherAsh,* so I don't try to rush or force a clearing before it naturally arises from my own inner wisdom. Those types of transformations are the ones that stick, rather than the forced "I just want to be done with this!" wishing that often ends up putting the issue underground, because it *will* rearise later.

### Questions to Ask Yourself:

How can I creatively bring my intent to this story? Is there any way I am still wanting someone else to change?

How can I let go? Is there any way I am still wanting Life to be different? How can I let go? What is a more empowering/healing way to look at this story?

Now, how specifically do you bring your intent and truth into the Story and Feeling Chambers? What is the next step? You are going to go forward listening to the guidance of your intent and looking for signs and insights on what to do next.

The following scenario is a continuation of the broken-vase story from chapter 1. Put yourself in her shoes as you read this example. Note that as the younger sister, you do not have to remember the initial event; you just have to explore your reaction, story, truth, and intent and then bring your intent and truth back into the Story Chamber to discover your next steps in healing. See how your intent will guide you.

Imagine if you are upset with your mother for not calling you on your birthday, but instead she calls you the next day to talk about your sibling's success. You are furious at her but don't know what to do. So you go through the chambers: You feel your fury and notice there is a strong desire of wanting your mother's approval and a sense of hopelessness and despair. In the Story Chamber, you find you have always told yourself the story that you are not as good as your sister, and that you will never measure up. Truth Chamber: You and your sister are very different.

Now I want to play with how you would respond differently with two divergent intents.

### LET'S SAY YOUR INTENT IS SELF-LOVE

Imagine holding the hand of self-love and walking back into the Truth Chamber: *My sister and I are very different.* Now enter the Story Chamber and explore how you perceive your story differently. You realize that your mother always favored your sibling (but now that doesn't hurt; you just see the truth) and how your grandmother also favored her eldest child over your mother. You see that your sister is not happy in her life, but you are content with who you are becoming, despite your mother's lack of support.

Then you name your intent (self-love) and ask what your next step is. You see that you can build your self-love by not fighting to get your mother's approval; instead, you appreciate yourself and name your strengths. A few days later, you get an inner message that you should spend more time with another mother figure in your life that loves you for who you are.

The next time your mother calls, before you pick up the phone, you consciously put one hand on your heart and one hand on your belly and say to yourself, *I love you, I don't need her to approve of me, I approve of you.* . . .

### LET'S SAY YOUR INTENT IS HONESTY

Imagine holding the hand of honesty and walking back into the Truth Chamber: *My sister and I are very different.* Now enter the Story Chamber and explore how you perceive your story differently.

Here you would name your intent (honesty) and ask what your next step is. You see that you have always been meek and quiet around your mother and your sibling, hoping that they will like you if you are a "nice girl." You see how being a "nice girl" has caused you to never speak your truth and to try to please everyone around you. With your new intent of honesty, you decide it is time to change your "nice girl" story and start to speak up. You know this will be challenging, so you commit to finding a teacher or a therapist or reading books on using your voice.

You can see how your intent tunes you into different parts of the story and helps you take new action. As you continue to listen, you'll keep getting inner messages and inspired ideas on how to continue unraveling the story. Keep listening and experimenting with new ways of being.

And remember: Your story may not give up without a fight. Your story may want to bury your awareness in the rubble of shame, blame, and judgment. Resist its siren call. Stay true to your intent.

### Four Ways to Come Back to Your Intent When Your Story Grabs Your Attention:

1. Say out loud, "Hi, Story! Good job, you got me again! Now I'm going to shift my attention."

   By naming the fact that your story caught you in its sticky drama, without judging yourself, you are taking your power back. Imagine that the story is like quicksand, and sometimes you are going to be swallowed up by it. Don't struggle, as that will only bury you faster. Instead, get quiet and look around for the hand of truth to help pull you out. Ask yourself, *What do I know is true here?* Then remind yourself of your intent. Put all of your attention on the feeling sense of your intent so that you are experiencing it in your body and not just thinking about it.

2. Ask yourself, *What would xxx do here?* and insert your intent into the sentence.

   So, for example, if your intent is "clarity," ask

yourself, *What would clarity do here? What would help me to gain more clarity?* Let the answer arise rather than trying to force it. Practice living with the questions, knowing that the answers will come.

3. Go deeper. Challenge yourself to look at your story again and see what earlier childhood story might be at play, or even older ancestral story.

   Often the story we are getting hooked by is only the tip of a much older story line. Our inability to unhook from it is because we think the attachment and suffering are coming from our present situation, when in fact the real barb is grabbing us from further back in the past. Look at the usual suspects: your relationship with your mother or your father, siblings, past trauma, or a past relationship that you are still healing from. Also, be willing to go back beyond your lifetime to other story lines you may be carrying forward from your ancestors (genocide, slavery, persecution, guilt, shame).

4. Step back into the Feeling Chamber and take a few minutes to simply be with your emotions, with no story.

   Sometimes while you are going back through the chambers, you may uncover a cache of unfelt emotions. Or you may have unintentionally merged your emotions and your story once again, and you need to separate the two so that you can regain clarity. If you are finding yourself spinning in your story, go back into the Feeling Chamber and check in with what you are feeling.

For example, if when you go from the Truth (in our example: *My mother always favored my sister*) to the Story Chamber and you find that instead of being able to witness that truth and how it has played out in your life, you have a huge reaction and are upset around how unfair and damaging the story was, then it's time to go back to the Feeling Chamber and practice separating out the Feelings from the Story. Put a hand on your heart. Let yourself have your feelings. Cry, grieve, feel. Let that little kid express. And then do your work of bringing your intent into the Story Chamber.

Don't try to bury those emotions, but don't hang out in the Story Chamber spiraling into more and more upset. Let your emotions arise. Do your best not to let the story interfere; just feel. Then go back to the Intent and Truth Chambers before you enter the Story Chamber. See if this helps you have more perspective about the story you are telling yourself.

In the next chapter, you will learn a very important Warrior Heart tool called *stalking*. Stalking teaches you specific ways to witness and untangle your stories and feelings. But first, let's explore how to honor your feelings at a deeper level.

## Honoring Your Feelings; Staying Out of Story

As you can see, the Warrior Heart practice will continue to help you get free of your story as you continue to dialogue with your intent and stay in your truth.

For each session of the practice, you want to go from Feeling to Story, Truth to Intent, and then back again, completing the full cycle in the Feeling Chamber.

Please don't stop in the Story Chamber and then feel you are done even if you have a great insight or bright clarity around your story. You want to end in a nonverbal place of your emotions rather than in the verbal world of your story. Your emotions, separate from your story, are a more reliable place to get information about your inner state of being.

Now, just like with your story, there is no "right" or "wrong" experience. You may go back into the Feeling Chamber and feel content, happy, peaceful. Or you may go back into the Feeling Chamber and feel grief, anger, or any other shade of emotion. What you find in the Feeling Chamber does not show you if you did the practice correctly (if I'm happy, I did it right; if I'm still upset, I did it wrong...). What you find in the Feeling Chamber just shows where you are in your personal process.

Being with your emotions is a powerful form of self-intimacy, a way to listen to the deepest part of yourself and honor what is there. You'll get to see if you are complete with the story for now, or if there are still more layers to work with. Releasing your attachment to one part of your story allows the next layer of emotions to arise, to be held and cleared.

### Pamela: High Blood Pressure Resolved

I noticed that I was getting high blood pressure when thinking about my current conflict with my father (an alcoholic) and when my sister continues to text me to make up with him.

I also started getting high blood pressure at work when the woman who sits behind me at work started bullying me. The overt bullying has resolved, but I continued to feel PTSD symptoms like high blood pressure whenever we were both in the office, even though we basically ignored each other from then on.

I noticed even whenever I started thinking about either of these stressful issues, I would also trigger high blood pressure. I tried deep breathing and other techniques to lower it but had difficulty stopping it once it was triggered. The worst part was trying to sleep after it had been triggered. I could feel the pulsing so strong, it really made it hard to sleep. I have been meditating since the '80s, but even meditation didn't help much. I don't believe in taking medication, and so was seeking natural approaches.

Luckily, I heard your technique just in time!

I did your Warrior Heart technique/meditation for both situations.

I only did it one time for each issue. I feel finally distanced enough from those issues that I no longer trigger high blood pressure from these stressful situations or thinking about them like I did before. In fact, I haven't had a reactive high blood pressure episode since then, and I have also been sleeping better.

When you feel resistance, this is your Little Soul's desire to understand or fix the issue you are working with. This is why it is so important to always end your Warrior Heart practice with the Feeling Chamber, and then learn to use your emotions as your guide for your next healing step going forward.

You are probably used to (often unconsciously) listening to the voices in your head, believing the story you are telling yourself, and then acting based on false information. Your story keeps you out of the truth and is often a cover-up for older, unprocessed emotions.

As you do the Warrior Heart practice regularly, you'll discover how often your mind leads you astray, and you'll begin to pay more attention to how you are feeling rather than what you are thinking. You'll question your thoughts and lovingly separate out emotions from story. With less story hooking your attention, you'll find you are more present in the moment. You'll also be more courageous in staying with your emotions, which will also bring you more into your body and your current experience. Instead of living only in your head, your body, mind, and emotions will be more integrated.

Your emotional body is a tremendous guide from this integrated place. You'll easily be able to notice when you are feeling "off" or triggered, and then you'll be able to name the sensations in your body. Your emotional body will become like an alarm that will let you know when something is brewing under the surface that needs your attention, or when your thoughts are misaligned.

Instead of diverting your attention or distracting yourself to avoid what you are feeling, you'll turn toward the feeling and get curious.

> *My belly is tight. My heart is racing. I'm feeling really scared right now. I'm not sure what is going on, but I'm feeling wobbly right now. I'm going to explore what I am actually feeling.*

If your emotional body could talk to you, here is what it might be saying:

> *I'm scared of being vulnerable in this situation. That person's actions just hurt me and triggered my old abandonment* fears. *Something*

*doesn't feel right in this situation; I'm not sure if what is being presented
is actually the truth. I'm still hurting from my relationship ending, and
I need more time to grieve.*

The story you are telling yourself is causing you to suffer
needlessly. Please go and look at the story!

When you show up with your emotional body with compassion and presence, you can then more easily explore what your
being needs to come back into alignment with your intent.

I've also discovered that when I revisit the Story Chamber,
there are times when I get a cognitive understanding of a piece
of my story, but the emotions are still running through my
body. When I simply let the feelings be there and compassionately hold them, they often dissolve on their own eventually.
Or when I stop thinking about how I want the story to be different, I have a more embodied understanding of what is really
going on, and then suddenly I see the piece I was missing. This
sometimes happens days after I've been working on a specific
issue.

Your new compassionate relationship with your emotional
body will allow you to stop being swamped by either your emotions or your story, because you will be open to them in the present. I've often found that my emotional body becomes really
loud as a way of getting my attention when I am not listening.
Keep asking your emotional body what it needs from you and
nourish it accordingly. Then keep watching your mind. Be a
Warrior of the Heart and do not allow your thoughts and beliefs to drag you back into suffering!

The Warrior Heart practice is not something that you will
do once and then be done. You may take the same issue through

the chambers several times, or you may find you only need one round to help you release your pain and struggle. Each time you bring an issue to the Warrior Heart practice, you'll find more freedom, more self-intimacy, and more compassion for your human experience.

The personal examples I've shared come from a place where I am dedicated to stalking myself and tracking my emotions, thoughts, and physical body work. I don't believe the work of getting to know ourselves is ever over; our life can be a grand adventure of expanding self-intimacy, self-respect, and self-love that spills over to deep respect and love for all beings. Sometimes the inner work is hard, emotional, and messy—like wading through molasses, and sometimes it is sweet and light like biting into soft cream-filled chocolate. Your new relationship with self takes learning to see yourself fully, honestly, and without your normal filters and recognizing that *everything* in your life is an opportunity for self-reflection and self-growth.

## *Review*

### Integration Questions

- How can I creatively bring my intent to this story?
- Is there any way I am still wanting someone else to change? How can I let go?
- Is there any way I am still wanting Life to be different? How can I let go?
- What is a more empowering/healing way to look at this story?

# Integration Practices

### Integrating the Chambers

Look back at your journal or artwork about how you imagine each of the four chambers. Using the Warrior Heart practice sheet, write or draw or paste pictures for each of the chambers, so you have a visual representation of how you experience them.

### Journaling

Freewrite, without thought or editing, your journey back through the chambers from your Intent. How does your choice of intent affect your perception of your story? When you step back into the Feeling Chamber, what is the tone of your emotional body?

### Creating a Chamber Board

One of my students was so inspired when she learned the chambers practice that she went home and created a three-dimensional representation of the chambers. She used a cloth as the base, on which she sewed four different-colored circles for each of the chambers. Then she created a felt doll representation of herself that she could move from chamber to chamber. In each chamber, she would ask the doll—which represented her Little Soul—questions and see how it responded. Physically moving the doll through each room gave her a distance that helped her to gain more insights and change old patterns.

You can create your own three-dimensional model of the chambers using paper, cloth, cardboard, seashells, or rocks. It can be a tiny, foldable creation or a room with masking tape on the floor to divide the chambers and furniture/pillows/statues/

artwork in each of the four quadrants. The only limit is your imagination.

### Story Play

Since it is our mind on high alert and our false but insistent stories that cause us to struggle, healing comes when we learn how to play and find humor in our stories. Remember my description in chapter 4 of Julie the Judge and Victor the Victim? In your journal, write down some funny descriptions for the main aspects of your story. If your Story Chamber and all of the characters within it were a comedy, how would you characterize each of the players in a silly, exaggerated way? Draw or describe each of the different actors in your internal play so you can begin to witness them with a fondness for their bumbling, earnest ways.

### Getting Your Ph.D.

What new truth can you write about what your current lesson is? Review your story, truth, and intent and then fill in this blank:

The universe loves me so much, it is giving me a Ph.D. in

_____.

## 8

# The Art of Stalking Yourself

*The very first principle of stalking is that a warrior stalks her/
himself, don Juan said. S/he stalks her/himself ruthlessly,
cunningly, patiently, and sweetly. There are four steps to
learning it: Ruthlessness should not be harshness, cunning should
not be cruelty, patience should not be negligence, and sweetness
should not be foolishness. These four steps have to be practiced
and perfected until they are so smooth they are unnoticeable.*

—CARLOS CASTANEDA

IMAGINE WHAT IT WOULD BE like if you knew your emotional, mental, and physical being so well that anytime something triggered you or upset you, you could quickly determine
what the source was, why you were feeling the way you were feeling, and what your next action to clean it up was.

As I first began to learn the Toltec teachings, I felt my mind
was about as peaceful as a hoarder's house after a tornado.
My thoughts, emotions, and reactions were so jumbled that I
couldn't sense what belonged to the present, what was from the
past, and what was someone else's story or belief that I had
picked up along the way.

You'll probably notice that when you first enter your Story Chamber, it is often hard to see the intricacies of the story because everything is tangled together. Something from your past is stashed in the back of the closet, along with a current difficult situation and an old story you can't let go of. When you aren't paying attention, your stories will seek out company, and they often go wandering around finding stories from the past and worries from the future to pal around with. Something that stands alone might be easy to recognize as an old agreement, such as fear, which takes on much larger proportions and weight when unconsciously linked to other stories from your past or present.

For example, your teammate's suicide when you were a teenager, your current friend's depression, and your story of why your mother abandoned you can be all piled together and making you feel miserable without knowing exactly why.

Every day, your reactions and stories give you the opportunity to either diminish or enhance your awareness. With every story that you believe without question, for every time you get stuck in shame or blame or guilt, for every repressed emotion, your awareness is narrowed down into a funnel of self-pity or self-importance. Your stories keep you in the lie of separation: "I'm worse than everyone else or I'm better than everyone else."

With your narrowed and cluttered viewpoint, you cannot comprehend that you have any choice about how to react to your world or that other people could have different points of view.

As you can see, when your Little Soul is in charge without awareness, it fixates on the rules and agreements about how to stay safe, often keeping your emotions hidden underground. You are like a marionette, where the strings come up from the roots of your past and choreograph every response and action you take.

But as you claim your Warrior Heart, you'll begin to expand your perspective. Instead of living in the unconscious crowded basement of your tiny Feeling and Story Chambers, you'll realize that there is an entire level above where you can get a much more expanded and roomy view of your emotions and thoughts. Your awareness will help you understand that everything you feel and think is not the truth. You'll be able to bring your unconscious patterns and behaviors up into the light so that you can examine them.

Honing your awareness does not mean that the feelings and stories will go away instantaneously, but how you relate to them will change immensely.

With awareness, you will begin to get familiar with your storehouse of emotions and your library of repetitive thoughts. You'll be able to see them as separate entities. As you explore the different types and themes of stories in your Story Chamber, you'll be able to stop believing the drama and instead patiently and compassionately attend to untangling them.

The Warrior Heart practice is a specific form of one of the main Toltec awareness principles: the art of stalking yourself. The word *stalking* sometimes makes people shudder, as it has become associated with obsession and violence. But the true meaning of the word *stalking* is much older than our more familiar modern version, and it is a vital tool for a Warrior of the Heart.

Stalking will allow you to start to organize your thoughts and feelings so they each have their own place. You will begin to recognize themes of emotions and where they are located in your body when you are in the Feeling Chamber. You will learn to witness your stories as distinct expressions of your mind.

So what is stalking in regard to a Warrior of the Heart? And why is it so important to cultivate the authentic qualities of stalking yourself?

## *Stalking Defined*

Stalking is an awareness practice of witnessing your thoughts, energy, emotions, and physical body without judgment, comparison, repulsion, or fear. When we stalk ourselves, we cultivate the qualities of a hunter: perseverance, patience, and presence. We are curious about all the habits of our being, from how we react to difficult situations to what we do when we are in love; from how we feel when we wake up in the morning to what causes us to lose energy throughout the day.

We stalk with a soft heart and a clear mind, witnessing all the many aspects of ourselves—our judge, victim, fears, and self-importance—as we carefully watch our reactions and our resistance to them. Everything comes under the penetrating light of our awareness.

As a Warrior of the Heart, you constantly stalk your internal world: your thoughts, feelings, and responses. This means getting to know the being that you are now; not who you wish you were or who you think you are supposed to be, but instead you become fully intimate with all aspects of yourself in this moment.

Stalking yourself will help you track your reactions and thoughts down to deep core beliefs, which can sometimes be preverbal, passed down from generation to generation, or integrated into our family or society to such a degree that we don't question their validity. This is why it can be so difficult to change core patterns even after years of therapy, teachings, and support—they can become completely woven into the fabric of our being, where we are unable to separate out what our essence is from what is a fundamental agreement we took on at a very young age.

Through your increasing awareness, you will discover that the way in which you respond to the experiences in your life creates your reality.

Let me take a moment here to clarify something. In recent years, Toltec teachings have sometimes been connected to the law of attraction because there are some similarities. The law of attraction, popularized by the movie *The Secret*, says that whatever state we are in attracts like experience. If we are in a positive state, we attract positive experiences, and if we are in a negative state, we attract negative experiences.

While there is truth to the law of attraction teachings, I've seen many people use it against themselves (or others) in an unhelpful way. Over the years, I've heard people say things like, "I just found out I have cancer, and I'm trying to figure out what I did wrong to make this happen," and "Well, of course they got in that car accident; they were so negative and depressed, they caused it to happen."

So the message you receive is: If you are happy-positive-loving all the time, then nothing bad will ever happen to you. Or if you are negative, the "bad" things that happen in your life are your fault and you deserve them.

This kind of new age spiritualism can be incredibly damaging and confusing because it can make us believe we are in charge of the universe and that if we live "right," we can avoid loss, betrayal, and all difficult situations.

Toltec philosophy holds that we are each dreaming our reality and that what we have control over is not necessarily *what* happens to us but rather how we *perceive* and use our experiences. In other words, we can "dream" through the eyes of the judge or the victim or through the eyes of a warrior. When we perceive the world through the lens of judge/victim, then everything that happens to us is good or bad, right or wrong. But for a Warrior of the Heart, everything that arises is an opportunity to increase our awareness, presence, and love.

There are probably many ways you currently stalk yourself that is not true Warrior Heart stalking, which I consider a crime against self. Like when you constantly berate yourself for your mistakes, gathering up each infraction with the precision of someone who is in control and out to get you. Or the ways you stalk your appearance and seek out your flaws in every mirror you look into. Or the soul-crushing habit of using everything against yourself when you imagine you are responding to other people's opinions, when in fact you are stalking and then projecting out your own internal negativity.

Most of us are better judgers than stalkers and are more familiar with being victims rather than warriors.

Here are some other ways our judge/victim can misuse stalking with others:

- Obsessively stalking those around us by constantly comparing ourselves to other people (whether in a magazine, movies, or in real life).
- Stalking others when we are determined to caretake or "save" them, and the action and behaviors of the person we believe we need to fix consume all of our attention.
- Try to do things "right" based on what we think someone else wants, and the ways we then stalk for evidence about how we should be or what we should do.

- And finally, we stalk others when we repeatedly ask the
  question *Do they love me?* and spend hours fantasizing,
  worrying, and looking for evidence that they are moving toward or away from us.

When we judge rather than truly stalk ourselves, we are critical rather than compassionate. Our internal dialogue is harsh
and unrelenting in pointing out what we are doing wrong or
how we should be different, and comparing ourselves to where
our judge thinks we "should" be. We are mean and berating to
ourselves and believe everything negative that happens is our
fault.

When we feel victimized, we believe the world is against
us and there is nothing we can do about it. We feel helpless,
alone, confused, and afraid. We feel no one understands us or
can support us, or we bond with other victims in a safe circle
of "poor us." It is always someone else's fault, and we have no
control.

When we are caught in the grip of the judge or the victim,
we often also project our viewpoint onto others by finding fault
or feeling sorry for the people around us.

The truth is that both our inner judge and inner victim are
constantly stalking for evidence that fits these points of view.
And when your attention is locked into this narrow band of
perception, it is very difficult to see that there is another reality.

In order to use stalking yourself as a way to gain information to support your transformation rather than a way to gather
information to punish yourself, you need to continually train
yourself to see through the eyes of love and curiosity. As we've
talked about throughout the chambers, the path of stalking
yourself starts with willingness.

## Cultivating Willingness and Curiosity

As don Juan says, "The basic difference between an ordinary person and a warrior is that a warrior takes everything as a challenge while an ordinary person takes everything as a blessing or a curse."

A Warrior of the Heart knows that all aspects of life are gifts to help us deepen our capacity to witness with love and act from our center. When we are willing to take full responsibility for our relationship with life (notice I said *full responsibility*, not *full blame* or *full punishment!*), we learn to face our experiences with equanimity, grace, and awe.

Here is another one of my favorite passages that don Juan taught his apprentice Carlos Castaneda: "For me the world is weird because it is stupendous, awesome, mysterious, unfathomable; my interest has been to convince you that you must assume responsibility for being here, in this marvelous world, in this marvelous desert, in this marvelous time. I want to convince you that you must learn to make every act count, since you are going to be here for only a short while, in fact, too short for witnessing all the marvels of it."

Your life is precious and fleeting, and the honor of witnessing all the marvels of life, including the wonder of the exquisite being that you are, is marvelous beyond words.

This is what it means to be a Warrior of the Heart, to willingly accept the challenge of claiming your life fully and embracing every opportunity to grow, learn, and transform.

Yet this is not an easy path. If you want a comfortable, stable, predictable life, then this path is not for you. To be a Warrior of the Heart means to constantly challenge your familiar limitations and perceptions, willingly dismantle your old stories, release stuck emotions, and step out of the false illusion that you are the center of the universe (or the equally misguided belief that you are insignificant or worthless).

Being a warrior stalking yourself is a path that demands great courage, willingness, and perseverance. The goal is to become wonderfully fluid and powerfully present in any given situation, and to give yourself the space and support to explore, make mistakes, and try again with each new opportunity. As a Warrior of the Heart, you will learn to go toward the mystery and the unknown with curiosity. Being a warrior stalking yourself doesn't mean you will never be afraid, or confused, or doubtful. In fact, sometimes you know you are on the path exactly because of these things.

What you are stalking are the old structures and beliefs that limit your perception and your experience. As you patiently stalk your reactions and calmly witness the voices in your head, you begin to map out the heavy weight of assigned false meaning and agreements that you hold.

## Brigit: Stalking a Story

I was going for a hike on my favorite nature trail, excited to finally be outside after a long week of work. But about fifteen minutes into my hike, I noticed that I felt off. Usually, I would try to power through and just enjoy my hike, but instead I started to stalk myself to see if I could figure out what was going on.

I went through the chambers quickly as I walked up a steep

part of the trail. I felt agitated and annoyed. There was no real reason in the moment of why I would be upset. I had just finished a huge project for work and my intent was for a weekend of relaxation. Here I was in my favorite national park, doing one of my favorite things. So what was going on?

I found a rock to sit on and started stalking myself, curious why I had gone from being happy to upset so quickly. I went back to the moment I turned in my report to my boss, and the feeling of elation and freedom. And then I noticed something I hadn't seen before: On my drive home from work, there was a little voice in my head that was saying, *You didn't do your best on that report. You could have done so much better. Your boss is going to make you do it over again, or she is going to give it to someone else who can do better. . . .*

Ah! As I witnessed myself, I saw how even though that voice in the car was just under my consciousness and I hadn't noticed it in the moment, my energy levels had plummeted and I felt defeated. I decided to keep stalking to see if there was an older story at play. *Where else have you felt defeated before?* I asked myself.

Immediately, I went back to a time in my childhood where I had turned in an art project I was really proud of, which was then graded against all the other kids in my class. I remembered standing in front of the wall of all our drawings later and realizing mine was not nearly as good as the other kids'. I felt ashamed and defeated. That was actually the last time I made art.

Once I had stalked the connection between my report and my experience as a kid, it was easy to separate them and tell myself the truth: I had done the best I could. My work was good, and I couldn't compare it to others. I was proud of myself and my accomplishments.

I jumped up and continued hiking, freed from the past and making a new agreement with myself to start doing more art as a way of expressing myself.

Here's the key: You don't need to know how; you only need to be willing to be present with yourself, be curious, and learn as you go along. As you get to know yourself more intimately, you'll begin to clearly know how to dissolve or break those beliefs that no longer serve you and create a new moral code for yourself.

I'll share more about the idea of a personal moral code later in this chapter, as it is one of the important acts of a warrior. But first I want us to deepen our understanding of stalking and the different ways we can stalk ourselves through the chambers.

## Claiming Your Warrior Spirit

Imagine large cats hunting their prey. They don't attack the second they see something move in the distance; big cats stalk their prey over days. They know where their prey sleeps, drinks, and feeds. Hunters are immensely patient, focused, and still. When they see opportunity, they act immediately, moving from stillness to pure action.

If you want to learn about some of the main qualities of stalking, watch videos of jaguars or lions hunting, or closer to home, spend time watching domestic cats. Domestic cats are consummate stalkers and excellent teachers.

Have you ever watched a cat stalk its prey and only bring 50 percent of its awareness and attention to what it is stalking? Neither have I! Cats constantly bring 100 percent of themselves to the task in front of them, whether that is stalking a bird in the yard or a feather on the end of a stick. And if they miss their intended target, they stop, regroup, and start again with 100 percent of their attention.

The Toltecs call this *jaguar stalking*. Jaguars are all about action; they stalk by seeking out their prey. When you use jaguar stalking, you take conscious actions in your life to unearth your beliefs and agreements.

Another form of stalking is *eagle stalking*. Eagles hunt by flying high above the earth and then swiftly diving down when they see their prey. When you use eagle stalking, you look at your life from a distance, mapping out the terrain to look for patterns and habits.

The third form of stalking is *spider stalking*. Spiders stalk by building a web and waiting for their prey to come to them. When you use spider stalking, you get really still and watch and wait for what you want to learn about yourself to come to you.

Each of us will resonate more with a particular type of stalking. No matter which of these forms of stalking you are most drawn to, it is important to learn the different languages and subtleties of the jaguar, eagle, and spider. Each is important in different areas of your life, and they can work together to help give you a whole picture of your inner structures.

As you become more skilled at stalking yourself, you can use all three stalking methods to see your patterns and habits, your thoughts and emotional reactions in a kind of holographic framework. This triple perspective then allows you to more skillfully dismantle the behaviors and beliefs of your past so that you can come into choice in the present.

For example, every quarter, I set aside time to stalk the previous three months. This helps me to gain information and insights about what worked and what did not work and what I want to create going forward. I start by stalking each month from an eagle perspective (vision). I step out of being "Heather-Ash" and imagine I am someone who is witnessing HeatherAsh from a distance. How is HeatherAsh in relation to herself and others? Is she getting enough alone time? Enough sleep? Is she feeling settled and calm? Is she finishing her projects on time or feeling behind? From the eagle's perspective, there is no judgment or a sense that things should be any certain way, only a wide-view exploration of any larger patterns that weave through my days.

Then I explore from the jaguar perspective (action). I honestly review every week, going through my calendar day by day and looking at how my choices and actions affected my life. This is not the cool distance of the eagle but the paws on the earth, what actually happened or didn't happen data gathering of the jaguar. I have to be willing to actively explore the consequences, both positive and negative, of my actions.

Finally, I connect to the wisdom of the spider (stillness). I get quiet and ask myself what my intent was for the previous quarter. What was I wanting for myself? What did I want to feel? What did I want to accomplish? Instead of looking at the patterns or naming the consequences, I ask a question and let the insights come to me. I don't search for these answers. Instead, I use these questions as a web, and I let the answers fly into my awareness over the following days.

All three perspectives help me to adjust as needed to create what I want moving forward.

As a Warrior of the Heart, you can practice stalking yourself every day, being guided by the clarity of the eagle, the confidence of the jaguar, and the patience of the spider.

Continually stalking yourself will show you where you have mis-invested your faith and energy: the places you have given other people power over your happiness, the places you are holding blame and victim, or the places you feel helpless or overwhelmed. As a stalker, you are on a journey to recover your faith in yourself. You are opening the door to the inner workings of your being and holding the willingness to change everything that no longer serves you.

Committing to change means committing to face fear. The spirit of a warrior isn't about not having fear; it is about learning how to face fear with an open heart and a relaxed body to create breakthroughs, not breakdowns. Remember, everything can be a wonderful challenge. The Warrior of the Heart faces obstacles with a smile and says, "You are a worthy obstacle!"

A warrior knows that every obstacle, when faced with courage and heart, can bring us more energy, freedom, and ultimately fluid choice as we dissolve the agreements connected to the obstacle before us—and in doing this, we reclaim our energy.

## Getting Clear: Stalking the Qualities of a Warrior of the Heart

Being a warrior means you are aware, responsible, and fluid. These are qualities that you dedicate yourself to cultivating over time as you would cultivate a garden.

Living as a warrior means living with failure, setbacks, mistakes, and uncertainty. You are not in an external war with anyone or anything; the battlefield is on the inside, and you are striving to reclaim your own respect, self-worth, and creativity.

What does it mean to be at war with the parasite in your mind? It means that you understand that your negative self-talk, low self-worth, anxiety, depression, and/or fearful living are draining your energy and enthusiasm. To be graphic, these things create a monster within you that drains your energy and will to thrive as effectively as a larval tarantula hawk that eats the insides of its spider host before it burrows out to become a full-grown tarantula hawk. The parasite within you is your Little Soul at its worst, trying desperately to control and keep you safe while destroying your peace of mind and happiness by eating you from the inside out.

Remember, as a warrior, you are not using hate to battle the Little Soul's desperate attempt at what it perceives to be its own survival. This is just another part of your Little Soul trying to gain control. It's like having a civil war, which appears as though we are fighting for change, but in truth it's about the victors re-creating the same oppression and dynamics as those who are in power.

No, we need to cultivate a different type of warrior—a warrior that is dedicated to using new qualities in every interaction with self and others.

By using a new code of conduct, we can help the Little Soul surrender into trust and reconnect with the Big Soul. This is not an easy fight, because the Little Soul is like a wounded, cornered animal trying to keep itself safe. Often when you approach, its claws are out and its teeth are bared. But with patience, creativity, and calm, you can gently teach the Little Soul that you come in peace and for healing. Anger will not create a bridge, nor will frustration. It is only your Big Soul patience, without judgment, that allows the Little Soul to begin to trust again.

Here are the two steps to moving from the parasitical Little Soul point of view to the expansiveness of the Big Soul's wisdom holding hands with your happy Little Soul.

### STEP 1: SHIFT YOUR ATTENTION FROM YOUR LITTLE SOUL'S FEAR TO YOUR BIG SOUL'S LOVE

Imagine a car with two gears: Little Soul and Big Soul. Take the gearshift and visualize moving it to your Big Soul perspective. Now close your eyes and go inside and imagine that you are stepping into the center of your Big Soul. Look at your current situation through your Big Soul eyes; with the compassion and unconditional love of a beloved grandparent. Dedicate yourself to releasing your Little Soul's fixed focus and following through on your Big Soul's intent.

### STEP 2: ALLOW YOUR BIG SOUL TO DIRECT YOUR LITTLE SOUL'S ACTIONS

Once you are clear on your Big Soul's intent, you will go back to the Story Chamber to work with shifting and releasing your Little Soul's hold on its story. We'll talk more about the how-to of reworking the Story Chamber in the next chapter. For now, part of your commitment to your intent is your willingness to work with your Little Soul.

Remember that when we set intent, both guidance and the obstacles start to show up. When you say (or proclaim) to the universe, for example, "My intent is peace," and follow that statement up with action (perhaps you start taking three deep breaths to find your peace before you speak, or you rearrange your bedroom so it feels more peaceful to you), Life will start giving you messages and signs to help you navigate more and more toward peace. Life will also show you where your obstacles to peace are. Yay!

In order to stay steady with our intent, despite discomfort or fear, we need to dream a new code of conduct for ourselves. We will not be able to bring our intent into our lives unless we dismantle the fear-based structure our Little Soul has built around our heart and wisdom.

Here are the seven sacred agreements of the Warrior Heart's code, which create a new dream of possibility and purpose:

- Radical responsibility
- Respect everyone
- Recapture your awareness
- Release the past
- Relax into the present
- Relearn creative play
- Remember gratitude

Let's go through the main characteristics that support the intent of a Heart Warrior and how to nurture them within you.

## The Warrior Heart Code

### RADICAL RESPONSIBILITY

*When you become fully responsible for your life, you can become fully human; once you become human, you may discover what it means to be a warrior.*

—DAN MILLMAN

A Warrior of the Heart claims their life as their work in progress. You take responsibility for your choices and actions, and especially for your mistakes. Taking responsibility does not mean you need to blame or judge yourself; you simply need to learn from your actions and reactions. Radical responsibility is one of the biggest gifts you can give yourself, because it allows you to change what is not working for you. This does not occur by changing anyone else but by changing your perspective and taking new actions.

### RESPECT EVERYONE

> *Give to every other human being every right*
> *that you claim for yourself.*
>
> —Thomas Paine

A Warrior of the Heart respects every human's choice, including their own. This means you don't let others hurt, abuse, or cross your boundaries; you respect yourself enough not to allow others to cross your own lines. This tenet of respect goes for everyone: Respect other people's right to their own opinions, respect others' right to make their own mistakes, respect other people's choices. You don't have to like their behavior; you can simply respect that they are a fellow human being who has the same basic desires as you—to be loved, to love, to feel safe.

### RECAPTURE YOUR AWARENESS

> *Rather than being your thoughts and emotions,*
> *be the awareness behind them.*
>
> —Eckhart Tolle

It is critical that, along with taking responsibility and building your self-respect, you also recapture your own awareness. It is only through awareness that you can take action on your intent. After you have acknowledged and experienced the Story and Feeling Chambers, you then move into the Truth and Intent Chambers. Here you will learn how to firmly link yourself to the vast spacious awareness that always surrounds and permeates your thoughts and emotions.

One great way to recapture your awareness is by noticing where you are emotionally overwhelmed or triggered around a feeling or a story and come back to your breath. Imagine you can take three steps back. Now open your awareness to everything around you: colors, shapes, sounds, and smells.

## RELEASE THE PAST

*The lack of mindfulness often makes us carry the unnecessary*
*possessions, stale ideologies, and rotten relationships along,*
*which unnecessarily clutter our lives and consciousness,*
*and stagnate our growth.*

—BANANI RAY

A Warrior of the Heart is committed to releasing any burdens and heaviness from the past. When you can't put down the clutter of what came before you, you are punishing yourself or feeling ashamed for things that no longer exist. Holding on to them takes valuable energy and time. It is not easy to clear the ghosts of the past, but little by little, you can open your hands and release the hurt and struggles and let them finally be laid to rest.

## Angela: Clearing Story, Clearing Emotions

I am at our apprenticeship gathering and heading out to HeatherAsh's property to build a sweat lodge. I am feeling excited, open, and honored to be a part of the first ceremony taking place on her property with our group.

As we start, my head fills with stories of my husband, whom I have recently separated from. Acknowledging this is the first sweat lodge I have participated in without him. *He would have loved this part; we did this part differently; this was the first place he told me he loved me. . . .* My brain created stories around all aspects of how the ceremony was being created.

Creating awareness around the fact that I was in the Story Chamber, I took myself to the creek, found a rock in the middle of the rushing water, and sat on it with my feet in the water. Allowing myself to sit in the Feeling Chamber, I dropped into my emotional body and allowed my grief to pour out, into the water, and down the creek. I allowed the tears to fall, allowing my grief to freely flow.

When my emotional body found stillness, I moved into the Truth Chamber. *In this moment, I am breathing, and my feet are really cold.* When I tried to dig for more truths, I would end up back in the Story Chamber. I chose to honor that there wasn't enough unraveling of my emotions yet and honored my present truth: my feet were cold in the creek. Period. That was my truth in that moment.

Moving into the Intent Chamber, I chose love. To move through this process with an open heart, to allow myself to give and receive love throughout this magical day.

After setting my intent, I stood up and joined in with our group. Very shortly, I witnessed I was in the Story Chamber again. I stood still and witnessed myself as the story grew bigger and bigger like a wildfire.

I was unable to stay present, so I gently took myself back to the creek, made the choice to sit in the Feeling Chamber. The tears fell quickly as my body understood what sitting in the creek meant now. I stayed with myself and used the water element to allow my grief to once again be carried away. It cleared quicker this time, and when I felt stillness settle in, I would move back to the group.

This process between the Story Chamber with the group and Feeling Chamber in the creek cycled close to a dozen times before I could consistently stay with the group.

## RELAX INTO THE PRESENT

*In every crisis, doubt or confusion, take the higher path—the path of compassion, courage, understanding, and love.*

—Amit Ray

If you look at any professional athlete, you'll see that they are totally present, relaxed, and ready for anything. Highly trained athletes are warriors, and the best of them seek to achieve a personal best in every moment. They are not thinking about past defeats or future wins. They are fully embodied in this present moment, knees bent and eyes up.

Imagine what it would feel to be completely relaxed and present in your life at all times. You would be alert without being wary, available without leaning forward into the next moment or falling back into the past, and softly ready for anything that may arise. You would be at choice about where your thoughts went. This is the warrior's stance of relaxing into the present.

### RELEARN CREATIVE PLAY

> *I've missed more than nine thousand shots in my career. I've lost almost three hundred games; twenty-six times, I've been trusted to take the game-winning shot and missed. I've failed over and over and over again in my life. And that is why I succeed.*

—MICHAEL JORDAN

So often, our fear of failure keeps us from succeeding. A Warrior of the Heart embraces failures, mistakes, and mishaps as fabulous learning experiences. Instead of responding to failure with despair, we respond with the delight of a child learning something new. Mistakes are the best invitation for harnessing your buried creativity. If you can face each mistake as part of a larger game, you'll discover the joy of "try again!" When you get excited at your next mistake, you'll know you are walking a warrior's path.

### REMEMBER GRATITUDE

> *How would your life be different if . . . You stopped focusing on what you didn't want and started focusing on what you do want? Let today be the day . . . You establish a clear intent, make a plan, and take actions toward your intent.*

—STEVE MARABOLI

A Warrior of the Heart remembers gratitude, regardless of circumstances. As you set your intent, name all the things you are grateful for in the situation you are in or in your life in general.

Part of setting intent is to focus your attention toward what is working, and gratitude is the best way forward.

The best attitude to have, along with the Warrior Heart's code, is curiosity. Be curious about how Life is going to help you manifest your intent. Be patient. Be persistent. And embrace the unknown!

As a Warrior of the Heart, you will always be ready for both the gifts and the challenges and be open to the unexpected. Have your tools always ready at hand: The seven sacred Warrior Heart agreements supporting you and the four chambers always available to help you untangle your present struggles and unweave your past stories.

## Review

### STALKING YOUR INTENT

Once you set your Intent in the Warrior Heart practice, you must stalk how you will bring it into your day. This means patiently, actively, and openly watching where you are able to stay in your Intent and where you get knocked out of it. *Ah, now I'm able to hold my compassion with my ex-partner. Ah, now I have lost any connection to compassion and I want to hurt her like I perceive she is hurting me.* You will also learn how to bring your Intent toward yourself: *How can I be compassionate toward myself for not feeling compassionate toward my ex in this moment?*

When you set an Intent, stalking allows you to sort where your work lies. When you can name where you can hold your Intent and where you struggle, you can be creative in how to support yourself when taking new action based from your Intent. Remember, solid, small, doable steps, warriors.

# Stalking Practices

### Building Your Own Moral Code

In addition to the seven new agreements of our Warrior Heart's code, I believe every warrior should create their own personalized moral code. Your moral code is three (or more) agreements that you commit to following in your own life. You know you will make mistakes, and you are dedicated to learning and growing as you integrate your moral code.

The Warrior Heart Code is:

1. Radical responsibility 2. Respect everyone 3. Recapture your awareness 4. Release the past 5. Relax into the present 6. Relearn creative play 7. Remember gratitude

Now create three more individual agreements that you will add to the Warrior Heart code to make it your own.

Here are some examples from my Warrior Goddess Facilitator Trainers, whom I invite to create their own moral code during their training. Notice how different they all are; some are short and to the point while others are more descriptive. You can use these to inspire you to craft your own moral code. Don't expect yourself to do this at one sitting; take your time really being with what your values are and how you want to conduct your actions as a Warrior of the Heart.

1. Always give myself support and love.
2. Treat everyone with respect.

3. Consider the impact of my words and actions upon others, and choose them with thought.

1. Always remember Divinity is within me and to trust that inner voice that speaks, even and especially when it's against the grain.
2. To embrace change, as change is my friend and saving grace.
3. Be gentle and compassionate with myself (even when it proves difficult).

1. I will be responsible for my own happiness.
2. Every day, I will do something that feeds my soul.
3. I will not react from an emotional place and will be impeccable with my words.

1. To *be* and to *act* positively and make positive *I am* and *I can* statements.
2. To love and support myself physically, mentally, emotionally, and spiritually and extend that love and support to others.
3. To speak my truth and live authentically with honesty, compassion, and discernment.

1. I hold myself and others in Love.
2. I maintain a consistent, strong connection to the universe and my guides.
3. I work to support and advocate for the underprivileged, alienated, and exploited. This includes humans, animals, and the earth.

1. I will be kind to myself and others.
2. I will stand up for what is right and true, defending others until they can protect themselves.
3. I will set a positive example for my son by living authentically.

1. Always come from a place of integrity.
2. Be authentic at all times.
3. Come from a place of love and nonjudgment when working with myself and with others.

### Stalking a Specific Topic

One highly beneficial way to use your stalking is to pick one topic on which you will hone your awareness over time. For example, I once spent a year stalking my own guilt. I dedicated myself to learning when and why I felt guilty. When I first started, I had to let go of my own beliefs around guilt and just stalk what was actually happening in my relationship with guilt. What I learned surprised me and allowed me to untangle the thread of guilt that used to wind painfully through my life, to the point that I almost never experience it.

To stalk a specific topic, first get clear about what emotion, experience, or thing you want to stalk. Then name how long you are going to stalk it for. (You can always extend your time frame if needed.)

Here are some examples of things you can stalk:

fear
discomfort
shyness
your relationship with your mother

your relationship with your father
your relationship with men or women
your anxiety about being in small spaces
shame
blame
guilt
being late all the time
expecting others to always be on time

When you stalk, remember that you are learning about your prey over time, not trying to figure it out all at once. It is often best to use a journal to keep track of what you learn, and do your best to not have expectations or ideas about anything. Come to your stalking as a newborn, free of thoughts, learning for the first time.

# 9

# Expansion

*Intent is a force that exists in the universe. When sorcerers*
*(those who live of the Source) beckon intent, it comes to them*
*and sets up the path for attainment, which means that sorcerers*
*always accomplish what they set out to do.*

—WAYNE W. DYER

MANY YEARS AGO, a friend said something that trans-
formed how I viewed myself and the spiritual/healing
path. Watching me as I forcefully tried to "fix" myself (I was
a warrior, dammit! I was stalking myself so I could stop being broken and start enjoying my life. I was miserable, but that
didn't matter. I was determined that all I needed was to try
harder!!!), he said to me, "HeatherAsh, you don't have to go
looking for problems. They will come to you."

What?!?

I had taken the idea of stalking to an extreme, where I was
constantly looking for problems to fix. I was like an artist who
constantly finds fault in their artwork and was always frustrated
and hopeless. The truth is my Little Soul had gotten ahold of

the idea of stalking myself, and I was now using it against me. I was more like an amateur hunter crashing through the forest rather than a seasoned stalker patiently and with great stillness pursuing their prey.

Remember that stalking yourself and the Warrior Heart practice are for creating more stillness, peace, and joy in your life. Please do your best not to do what I did, which is to use the tools as another way to make yourself feel miserable. Stalking is different from judging. The Warrior Heart practice is a way to untangle into more love instead of tightening the knots of fear. Surrender to your Big Soul and ask your inner wisdom to show you how to navigate each chamber.

Again, doing this work does not mean that the challenges disappear magically from your life. The challenges are the challenges. But being a warrior instead of a worrier and coming from your heart instead of your mind changes everything.

When I first had the idea to write this book, I knew I wanted to bring it to a big New York publisher. I dearly loved my established publisher, so making the decision to relocate to New York was a hard choice. But a voice inside of me whispered that it was time to expand. I moved to New York City as a result of this inner guidance and began working with my agent to finish the forty-eight-page proposal for *Warrior Heart,* which had taken me five years to write.

It was an exciting time; four publishers wanted the book. Now I had to pick which one was the "right" publisher to midwife it into the world.

I agonized for days over the decision, undecided between two incredible people and publishing houses. After going through the chambers practice, my intent was faith.

On the day I had to give my decision, I woke up and prayed, asking for guidance. And I received an answer that surprised me: Go with the less experienced publisher.

The moment I told my agent my decision, I felt I had made a mistake.

But the decision was now made, and there was no turning back. For days I agonized . . . *I made the wrong decision! I just sabotaged my writing! The book is not going to get the support it needs!* But each time I tuned in, I kept hearing one word.

*Faith.*

One day, I said out loud, "I made the wrong decision, and you want me to have faith?" *Yes* was the answer that resonated through my being.

For weeks, I bounced between feeling confused and judgmental and trusting and open. Something would happen, and I'd think, *Ah, see? It is perfect!* I loved the publisher I had chosen, but there was still always an underlying feeling that I had made the "wrong" choice.

What this time did for me turned out to be a miracle. I let go of knowing what was right and what was wrong. I chose to trust the universe even though I knew I "should" have gone with the other publisher. I also knew I was being shown something really important.

I let go of my vision for the book, of my dreams, of my hopes, and in that letting go, I realized no matter what happened with the book, my life was great. I was giving my gift. My job was not to understand how it would be received or shepherded into the world; my job was to simply write the best book I could write and offer it up.

Then the publisher who had acquired my book left Simon & Schuster, and suddenly the book was orphaned.

This is an author's worst nightmare; the champion that brought your book into a publishing house would disappear, and your baby would be abandoned to whomever in the organization ended up having to pick up the screaming child and care for it, along with all their other (more loved and consciously chosen) children.

I panicked. "See, you did make the wrong decision!"

And again, I went back to my intent. Faith.

Again, I surrendered. I listened. I did not let myself go into story. I waited.

Stalking yourself is about constantly reconnecting your Little Soul to your Big Soul. Redirecting thoughts. Breathing through emotions. Untangling stories. Moving from fear to love, from crisis to faith.

One day, I woke up knowing the next action as clear as a mountain view on a sunshiny day. I wanted to go back to the other publisher that I had initially chosen not to go with. Getting into a publishing contract is difficult; getting out of one is just as difficult. And then having someone you said no to welcome you back . . . well, it was a long shot.

But this is exactly what happened. I was released from my contract. I was welcomed back to St. Martin's with open arms. And I felt my Big Soul smiling at me and saying, *See! Have faith.*

The way is not always clear. And sometimes you will be guided to take actions that may make no sense. But let your intent and not your mind be your guide. Hold hands tightly with your truth and your intent. They will guide you through the rocky landscape of your mind and teach you how to create a fertile, receptive garden where you can choose what you grow within.

## The Three Attentions

The transformation that comes from cleaning and connecting is not an even, all-at-once process but a spiral, back-and-forth practice that is unique to each of us. Some of your stories will be easy to dislodge from your psyche simply by bringing your attention to them, and some are as tenacious as a barnacle on a boat. When your Little Soul feels threatened or afraid, it often grips even more tightly to what it knows. And even in your work to create "better" agreements, you can inadvertently tie yourself in tighter knots.

We must keep stalking ourselves continuously to make sure we are actually cleaning and connecting rather than hiding our dirt and creating more separation with our mind.

To continue on our big-picture map of the Big Soul and Little Soul from chapter 1, here is another potent conceptual framework that can help you to stay on track: the first, second, and third attention.

The concept of the first, second, and third attention is an excellent way to understand our relationship to our stories.

## The First Attention

When we are in the first attention, we are living completely from our unconscious beliefs. Whatever we learned from our parents, or our peers, or our culture is considered the truth. There is no self-reflection or exploration; we live within the confines that are presented to us. There is no other reality.

An example of living in the first attention is someone who follows the religion they were raised in without questioning it, wears the clothes they believe they are supposed to wear, gets married and has children and becomes a doctor or lawyer because that is the only choice in their mind. They follow what is expected of them and expect the same of themselves (and often everyone around them). There is nothing wrong with the first attention; it is just based in following a role rather than following your heart or your passions. For some people, living in the first attention is fulfilling and effortless.

But for most of us, living in the first attention feels empty and is often filled with a sense of conflict because we are ignoring our own inner stirrings. And because we are not fluid in the first attention, but always following rules and roles, we are often judgmental toward others' choices and for not doing things the "right" way.

## The Second Attention

When we step into the second attention, our awareness opens and we recognize that we don't have to follow any specific path or role. We begin to challenge our own beliefs and thoughts, and we start to carve our own path. We understand that we can choose who and how we want to be. It is often an almost intoxicating time, because we understand we are free and powerful. It can also be scary, as we realize that what we thought was true is only a point of view, not a fixed reality.

When we step from the first attention to the second attention, we use our awareness and energy to re-create the entire dream of our lives. We might change religions, change our style and expression, choose to be single or marry into a different culture, or choose to pursue a totally different career. The danger of the second attention is that it can be easy to get stuck there and create an even more rigid cage for ourselves. Since we are for the first time consciously using our awareness to create our own structures and trajectory, we can fixate that this new way of being is not just a choice we are making but the "right" way to be. This is how people can become incredibly dogmatic and/or spiritually smug about things like veganism, spirituality, and politics. They have now invested their energy into a new structure, and instead of realizing it is a personal choice, they decide this is the new "correct" and only way to be.

Here's another way to talk about it. In the first attention, the Little Soul follows the rules so it feels safe. In the second attention, the Little Soul creates a whole new structure that it feels safe within. In both the first and second attention, who is doing the choosing is your Little Soul, and no matter how aware or hip your Little Soul is, its focus is always going to be on one thing: staying safe.

In the second attention, the most aware, spiritual, or healing-based people can be immensely judgmental, feel victimized by the world, and feel bitter that the world is not the way it "should" be.

And there is nothing more obnoxious or stifling to our growth than what I call *spiritual smugness*. This is a new form of the same old story, recycled to make it seem "spiritual."

The following came from a blog I wrote when I first started exploring the idea of spiritual smugness:

## On Spiritual Smugness

"Do you have a vegan option?" she asked the flight attendant. There was an underlying thread of iron in her voice, pulled taut across her vocal cords.

We were on a flight from Nashville to Austin, and the woman sitting by the window was somewhat agitated. The flight attendant cheerfully said, "I can give you a roll and jam, and would you like sugar with your tea?"

"Noooo sugar!" she replied with a hair-standing-on-end, head-shaking offense seeping through her words like rust.

I passed her my extra bread and sent a smile her way and then went back to my book.

It was when we landed that things got really interesting.

I reached up to get my suitcase from the bin above me, struggling with the weight. When the gentleman standing in the aisle walked past without helping, I felt fury rising behind me like smoke. "I cannot believe that!" my window companion said, thick, angry poison flowing with her words. "He is so rude! I can't believe he didn't help you. What is wrong with people?"

As she fumed, another man helped me and I was on my way, sending a blessing back toward my riled-up vegan that she might find peace.

I had two thoughts as I exited the plane. First, perhaps she didn't quite understand the message of the book she was reading, *Zen and the Art of Motorcycle Maintenance.* (Patience. Awareness. Fixing the little things as they arise with calm presence. If you haven't read the book, it's a classic.)

And second, spiritual smugness causes so much suffering.

One thing we rarely talk about is how even when we are "spiritual" or "evolved" or even "right," it does not give us license to lash out at other people, regardless of their behavior or beliefs; they are simply unconscious.

We are all unconscious at times. We all make mistakes. We all drop back into the first attention. And we all have a right to our beliefs and our actions. Respecting other people's choices, even when we don't like them, goes much further than any other position.

I used to be seriously spiritually smug. When I was in college and a political activist, I saw anyone who was not fighting for change as uneducated, unconscious, and part of the problem. I was fighting the good fight, and if you weren't with us, you were against us. Then I transferred that self-important attitude to my spiritual path—secretly believing that my spiritual friends and I were better than people that weren't on a path of awakening/bettering themselves/healing.

Sometimes I still fall into that trap. But the second I catch myself, I dig out of the quicksand of spiritual smugness as quickly as I can. That type of thinking leads to separation, anger, judgment, and a false sense of superiority that is like sugar; it may give you a boost in the short run, but it is detrimental in the long run.

Being spiritually smug makes us feel "right" for a time, which is a potent cocktail of false power. But the price is too high; we sacrifice our happiness, humility, and our humanness. When we believe ourselves to be better than others, or we hang on to our right to be angry or bitter or demeaning, regardless of others' behavior, we are eating anger, drinking bitterness, digesting distain. And we are usually doing exactly what we are accusing others of doing in some form.

My airplane neighbor was rudely accusing someone else of being rude. The man she was spewing her anger at was just making a choice not to help, for whatever reason. Perhaps he didn't notice me struggling. Or he was late for a flight connection. Or he had a bad back. Or he was unconscious. Or he didn't like women. Or . . . the reason doesn't matter, really. He chose not to. I could be offended, or hurt, or angry at his choice. Or I could honor his choice and move on with my day without tripping over my own fantasy of what life should look like.

I'm not saying this is easy. Recently, I had to do some serious deep breathing in order to refrain from ranting at a friend who was being super negative. There is no magic pill or meditation or holy place where you suddenly never react to anyone's actions. It takes practice, patience, and turning your attention away from other people's choices, and to hold a mirror up to see where you're being righteous or reactionary or resistant. Sometimes the reflection is painful, but it is always deeply healing to own our shadows. We can stop projecting them outward with our spiritual smugness or righteous rage or bountiful blame.

Be gentle with yourself and others.

Let's be the people who ooze love when we are squeezed by life rather than oozing hatred or frustration or smug superiority.

Spiritual smugness is one example of a way that we can sabotage our own progress toward inner freedom. Other ways include spiritual bypass (*Since I'm spiritual, I'm not supposed to have any messy emotions or stories, so I'm going to pretend I'm great and happy, no matter what*), getting caught in self-importance (when your Little Soul starts feeling that it is better than everyone else as a form of protection), or getting trapped in self-effacement (a false form of humility: thinking you are less valuable or less important than others).

How do you stay out of the traps of spiritual smugness or spiritual bypass?

Please never get complacent or assume that just because you've done some degree of healing/spiritual work that you should be "done." One thing I've learned never to say is, "Oh, I'm so glad I'm done with that!" because of how often the original story, or a version of it, comes back around, knocking at my door. I also pay attention to any place my Little Soul tries to tell me I shouldn't have "issues" any longer. I've found that the longer you are on a spiritual or healing path, the trickier it is to spot your Little Soul / ego-personality.

The truth is that it is incredibly difficult to break out of the second attention and into the third. The second attention is a powerful place for the Little Soul, and it feels like freedom. But it is only a step toward true freedom.

## The Third Attention

In the third attention, we transfer our awareness from the perspective of the Little Soul into the expanded wisdom of the Big Soul. We understand at a deep, nonverbal level that everything is a choice. Our Little Soul is not the center of our perception and actions; it is a secondary character that is now being inspired and directed by the Big Soul.

The more we attune to the third attention, the more fluid, good-natured, and happy we become. We know there is no "right" or "wrong" way to be. What I've found is that people who are immersed in the third attention do not use outside rules to guide their choices; they have an incredibly strong inner moral code that they follow, not because it is "right" but because they understand that every action has a consequence, and so every action is made deliberately.

If we go back to our Big Soul / Little Soul map, we have much work to do clearing the first attention energetic lines of agreements and beliefs that block our access to Big Soul. And if we truly want to be free, we also have to break our attachment to any new self-created agreements of the second attention. And as we have said, our work is twofold—a bringing together of our warrior focus and our heart expansion:

1. **Clean** using tools like the Warrior Heart practice to separate and untangle the knots of emotions and story that keep us trapped in a tiny world of drama and fear.
2. **Connect** with your Big Soul by doing things you love.

My experience is that it is best to do both these two actions simultaneously: clean and connect. I've met spiritual people who have spent their lives meditating and connecting to their Big Soul, but once they are off their yoga mat or their sitting pillow, they are immediately pulled back into their own inner drama and plagued by judgment. I've also met people who get narrowly focused on "fixing" themselves and are compromised by their Little Soul co-opting their attention. It would be like someone in a huge, glorious temple spending their time scrubbing the dirt under the chairs and never looking up at the light pouring through the stained glass windows.

Living in the third attention is living in the Intent and Truth Chambers, connected to your Big Soul. It is about learning to see without your eyes and listen without your ears. What I've found is that the more we clean, the easier it is to connect. The more we connect, the more inspired our cleaning becomes.

Annie Dillard beautifully expresses the feeling sense of living in the third attention in her prose poetry book *Pilgrim at Tinker Creek*. Please take a moment to get really quiet and let her words sink in and touch that nonverbal, Big Soul place within you.

The world's spiritual geniuses seem to discover universally that the mind's muddy river, this ceaseless flow of trivia and trash, cannot be dammed, and that trying to dam it is a waste of effort that might lead to madness. Instead you must allow the muddy river to flow unheeded in the dim channels of consciousness; you raise your sights; you look along it, mildly, acknowledging its presence without interest and gazing beyond into the realm of the real where subjects and objects rest purely, without utterance. "Launch into the deep," says Jacques Ellul, "and you shall see."

The secret of seeing is, then, the pearl of great price. If I thought he could teach me to find it and keep it forever I would stagger barefoot across a hundred deserts after any lunatic at all. But although the pearl may be found, it may not be sought. The literature of illumination reveals this above all: although it comes to those who wait for it, it is always, even to the most practiced and adept, a gift and a total surprise. I return from one walk knowing where the killdeer nests in the field by the creek and the hour the laurels bloom. I return from the same walk a day later scarcely knowing my own name. Litanies hum in my ears; my tongue flaps in my mouth Ailinon, alleluia! I cannot cause light; the most I can do is try to put myself in the path of its beam. It is possible, in deep space, to sail on solar wind. Light, be it particle or wave, has force; you rig a giant sail and go. The secret to seeing is to sail on solar wind. Hone and spread your spirit till you are yourself a sail, whetted, translucent, broadside to the merest puff.

In the second attention, we name and understand: We use our awareness to connect with the physical world by knowing where the killdeer nests or when the laurel blooms. We are confident, we are aligned, we are attuned to the rhythms and flows of nature and our place within it.

As you move from living between the lower Feeling and Story Chambers and begin to live more in the upper Truth and Intent Chambers, you'll find that you are able to consciously direct your dream. You will live more and more in the second attention, widening your awareness and understanding the great gift that your attention is. Instead of being hooked by the muddy waters of your mind, you'll be able to raise your sights and look toward the horizon, toward all possibility. You'll be able to choose where to rest your gaze. You will skillfully weave your intent throughout every interaction and recalibrate your emotions and story in alignment with your truth.

And yet there is more.

In the third attention, all words fail. Our Little Soul merges with our Big Soul, and we truly see the world as it is: as light dancing through everything. With this surrender of the Little Soul into the vastness of the Big Soul, we lose self-identity and separateness. We are the world, and the world is within us. We are a song being sung by the universe. We are the universe, open-throated, celebrating every molecule of existence with liquid sound. We are a sail, whetted, translucent, and ready for the breath of the Divine.

These moments of grace, when we completely forget our separate identification and remember our Divine connection, are what the Buddhists call "dipping into the stream." Beneath the muddy stream of Little Soul mind is the great expansive purity of our Big Soul river, which empties into the universal ocean of all. This is what we call the *nagual:* the place of pure possibility, pure potential, the place before manifestation. Everything created comes from the nagual; it is our source, the Big Soul of our Big Soul.

From the nagual comes the *tonal,* or all thought, concepts, and physical creation. We've been trained to keep our focus on the tonal, or on our physical experiences, stories, and manifestations. But this is only half of the picture.

Your Little Soul has hooked your attention for long enough. It is time to expand into the free-flow freedom and potential of your Big Soul. My prayer for all of us is that we have the courage and dedication and find the ever-important support of community to disconnect our Little Soul from its fears and need to control, and reconnect to the grace and grandeur of our Big Soul. Let's expand into the mystery of the third attention, while we embrace the parts of us that still cling to the first and second attention. Let's rest our consciousness in our Big Soul wisdom while we parent and guide our Little Soul back home.

As you dance and weave your way from the first to the second attention, and then from the second to the third, know that the path is not straight or easy. It will take a lifetime of practice, a tremendous amount of patience, and your warrior spirit combined with your biggest heart. Remind yourself: You are in for the long haul. And enjoy the journey, chamber by chamber. The key is not to strive for the third attention or try to force yourself toward your Big Soul but to systematically create the conditions to invite the light of awareness to shine through you.

Keep cleaning. Keep connecting. And keep choosing, again, to merge with all that is and all that ever will be.

You've got this, Warrior of the Heart.

Find discussion questions online at
Heatherashamara.com.

# Appendix

## *Glossary of Terms*

**Big Soul:** The aspect of your being that is connected to Life, God, Spirit. Your Big Soul is your unique ray of light that moves from lifetime to lifetime. Your Big Soul never feels separated or alone, and it is constantly shining love and acceptance, even when you can't perceive it.

**Little Soul:** The aspect of your being that feels separate and alone. Also called your *ego-personality,* your Little Soul starts off connected to your Big Soul, but over time begins to rely more on the rules and agreement it learns, which it believes will keep it safe.

**Agreements:** We make conscious and unconscious agreements. Conscious agreements are made intentionally. For example: "I will work at this job for this many hours and be compensated in this manner..." or "We agree in our relationship to be monogamous." Unconscious agreements are behaviors and beliefs that we pick up from our parents, peers, schools, religions, or society without realizing we are carrying them; or they are false thoughts we make up based on our experiences that become new "rules" of how we should behave or how the world is. For example, "I'm terrible at art because I didn't get recognized by the teacher," or "I'm not lovable, because my father left me and my mother when I was young," are examples of unconscious agreements that are formed through experiences or mirroring by the world around us. Our work is to bring the unconscious agreements up into our awareness so we can decide if they are serving or hindering us.

**Story:** A fantasy made up in the mind. A story can be beautiful and inspiring, or it can be damaging and draining. Harmful stories are a series of agreements that solidify into a false reality. A story can feel like the truth but be created in the mind based on false evidence or selective evidence gathering. As we become aware of our stories, we can begin to decide if they are opening us into more possibility or closing us down into more fear.

**Witness-self:** The aspect of yourself that can step out of the story and see other possibilities and truths. Your Big Soul is constantly witnessing your Little Soul, with no judgment or expectation. We align more with our Big Soul when we begin to not believe the stories and fears of our Little Soul but see them as passing phenomena that we can choose to simply be with rather than believe or act from.

**Intent:** Your focus, or 100 percent commitment to taking an action. Intent is also a force that moves through all of creation, and our job is to link our personal intent with this universal energy of intent.

**Not doings:** Action that you take for no reason and no reward, designed to help break up habitual patterns and help you become more fluid.

**Tonal:** The physical, manifest world, including concepts and thought.

**Nagual:** The invisible, unmanifest world, the energy before form or thought.

**First attention:** The first time you use your attention to create your reality. For most of us, the first attention is created by what we learn from our parents, teachers, religion, peers, and the society we live in. There is often not conscious choice involved, but a copying or reacting to what others are doing around us.

**Second attention:** When we realize we have the power and capacity to choose how we want to dream, or create our reality through our awareness. In the second attention, we begin to break down agreements and beliefs that don't serve us and consciously choose what we want to believe and how we want to see the world.

**Third attention:** While in the second attention we can sometimes get fixed as we make new rules for who or how we (or the world) should be, in the third attention, we are completely fluid with our awareness. We understand that everything is about perception and that perception is highly personal. We work toward responding to each situation not from our mind or agreements but from our connection to spirit and our own intuition and inner guidance.

**Petty tyrant:** Someone you perceive has the power (usually an authority figure or family member) to make your life miserable through their actions. Petty tyrants can be great gifts, for they mirror to us where we have given our sense of happiness and peace away to someone else and are using their behaviors to make ourselves miserable. It takes immense courage and self-reflection to move beyond the hooks of a petty tyrant (or to know when to walk away in self-love).

## Feelings

The more we gain emotional literacy, the more we can learn to name, feel, and let our emotions come and go. To deepen your ability to recognize and experience the many nuances of emotion, go to the internet and do a search for "faces of emotion chart" images. Print out one of these visual representations of emotions and put it on your fridge to help remind you to tune into the voice of your emotional body.

Also do an internet search for "list of emotions" to see the many different ways that researchers have characterized, named, and sorted human emotions. Below are four different methods of exploring emotions. As you read through these diverse theories of emotions, see what resonates with you. You can even make your own chart or index cards with images from magazines to expand your emotional vocabulary and get more comfortable with all expressions of your emotional body.

The detailed list below comes from Byron Katie's website and explores eight different types of emotional expression from when you are believing the story you are in, with gradations of

| Angry | Depressed | Confused | Helpless |
|---|---|---|---|
| irritated | lousy | upset | incapable |
| enraged | disappointed | doubtful | alone |
| hostile | discouraged | uncertain | paralyzed |
| insulting | ashamed | indecisive | fatigued |
| sore | powerless | perplexed | useless |
| annoyed | diminished | embarrassed | inferior |
| upset | guilty | hesitant | vulnerable |
| hateful | dissatisfied | shy | empty |
| unpleasant | miserable | stupefied | forced |
| offensive | detestable | disillusioned | hesitant |
| bitter | repugnant | unbelieving | despair |
| aggressive | despicable | skeptical | frustrated |
| resentful | disgusting | distrustful | distressed |
| inflamed | abominable | misgiving | woeful |
| provoked | terrible | lost | pathetic |
| incensed | in despair | unsure | tragic |
| infuriated | sulky | uneasy | in a stew |
| cross | bad | pessimistic | dominated |
| worked up | tense | | |
| boiling | | | |
| fuming | | | |
| indignant | | | |

| Indifferent | Afraid | Hurt | Sad |
|---|---|---|---|
| insensitive | fearful | crushed | tearful |
| dull | terrified | tormented | sorrowful |
| nonchalant | suspicious | deprived | pained |
| neutral | anxious | pained | grief-stricken |
| reserved | alarmed | tortured | anguished |
| weary | panic | dejected | desolate |
| bored | nervous | rejected | desperate |
| preoccupied | scared | injured | pessimistic |

| Indifferent | Afraid | Hurt | Sad |
|---|---|---|---|
| cold | worried | offended | unhappy |
| disinterested | frightened | afflicted | lonely |
| lifeless | timid | aching | grieved |
| | shaky | victimized | mournful |
| | restless | heartbroken | dismayed |
| | doubtful | agonized | |
| | threatened | appalled | |
| | cowardly | humiliated | |
| | quaking | wronged | |
| | menaced | alienated | |
| | wary | | |

each. Take some time to read through each column and high-light the emotions that are most familiar to you.

## Special Cases

Here are special cases in relation to the Warrior Heart practice: how to use the practice with kids and teenagers, if you have had trauma, you are in a relationship with someone (or you are that someone) with a mental health illness, or if you are dealing with a long-term physical illness.

### KIDS AND TEENAGERS

Whenever people ask me how they can make sure that their kids are happy or have strong self-worth, I always remind them that as a parent, you have three main jobs: express your love and appreciation for your children, remind them of their talents and gifts, and do your own work. So before you introduce the Warrior

Heart practice to your children, make sure that you have been doing the practice yourself for long enough that you have learned to separate out Feelings from Story and Story from Truth.

It can be very helpful with children to teach them to be literate with their emotions early on. Use a simple chart with cartoons or real faces. Real faces are best, especially for young children; pictures of the child himself or herself are even better. Using a mirror so that children can see their own face is a great tool (in play, not just when children have a charged emotion). You can also take pictures of different emotions and put them on the fridge, or use video. Kids love seeing themselves in pictures or videos, and it helps them to identify emotions in themselves. It is also important for parents to verbalize their own emotions in real-life contexts throughout the day.

You can make a game of picking one emotion each day to express and exaggerate. Kids are extremely fluid with their emotions, and if they are given permission to feel and then release their emotions, they will bring this ability to adulthood. Most of our problems with emotions as adults come from repressing or diverting them, so be mindful to give your kids the space to be emotional without shaming or trying to shut them down. You can teach children about where it's appropriate and where it is not appropriate to express emotions, but do this as a way to educate them rather than as a way to scold them. Again, having the child see the parent have emotions, feel them, and watch them pass is a great learning tool. It is really important to work with positive or neutral emotional states (happy, calm) not just charged negative ones.

You can introduce the Warrior Heart practice to your children as soon as they first learn to talk by asking them simple questions from the four chambers.

"How do you feel?" Once they share, acknowledge their feelings by repeating them back with compassion and presence. Kids learn basic emotions first (sad, mad, scared, happy, surprised, excited), so for young kids between two and five years old, you can ask questions like "You felt mad when your friend took your toy without asking?" or "You felt sad when your brother would not play with you?" You can then begin to help them define more complicated emotions as they get older: "You felt confused and upset when your friend didn't sit by you at lunch?" Wait to see if they have any other emotion they want to share. Then if it feels appropriate, you can then share an experience you had that was similar: "When a friend doesn't call or visit me, I sometimes feel sad and confused, too." You are not sharing to negate or trump their experience but to show them that you understand their feelings.

Then invite them to simply sit with their feelings: "Let's take one minute to simply be with the feelings of upset and confusion. I'll sit here with you."

My friend Angela Murphy is a speech-language pathologist and somatic experiencing practitioner who specializes in working with children. She has kids label the part of the body they feel the feeling in and helps them with describing with vocabulary before she has the child sit with it. She explains:

> You want them to be able to label where it is, how it feels, and then use the time to sit to watch and see what happens next and what changes. You are teaching them to track sensations and look for changes. You can have kids point to a body part that feels this way, use dolls, or use gingerbread cutouts with older kids to draw and talk about emotions.

Affirm it is okay to feel the feeling: "It is okay to feel sad. Would it be okay if I sit and feel the sad feeling with you for a minute? I will be here with you. You are safe. Can we sit for a minute and breathe and watch what happens to the sad feeling in your belly?" If the child is upset by this, remind them that feelings are always changing and that no feeling stays forever. It is very important for kids to know that they are not alone with their feelings and if they get too big that the parent is there to help them regulate and contain feelings that feel too big until they have the tools to do it themselves.

Remind them they don't need to do anything but simply sit and breathe and be with their feelings and watch them move. You can even set a timer for one minute (or more or less depending on the age of the child and their capacity to sit still). Angela also counsels:

It is just as important to have children sit with neutral (safe, calm, okay) or positive experiences as it is to sit with negative ones. It is very important to know what safe, calm, and okay feels like so that they can come back to these feelings when they are feeling more charged emotions.

Then ask them to describe what they noticed about the feeling. "Where did you feel the sadness in your body? Did it feel sticky or heavy or cold? Does it feel fast or slow? Warm? Heavy or light? Does it have a color, shape? How does feeling move?" If you ask them, they can often show you what the feeling looks like in body through a movement. "Show me what the feeling looks like." Help your child approach their emotions almost like an anthropologist; they are learning to both experience and explore the feelings within them. Give them examples and words to help them build a vocabulary, while doing your best not to project your thoughts of what they are experiencing onto them. Again, listen to their experience and help them go deeper in their understanding.

"What story are you telling yourself?" Early on, explain what a story is using an example from your own life. You can say things like: "A story is something we make up in our brains, even when we don't have all the information." You can help them explore the concept of a story versus real life. "Is that something you thought about or something that really happened?" Then give examples from your own life: "Last week, I made up a story that because your mom woke up grumpy, she must have been mad at me. But the truth was she was not upset with me; her head was hurting her really badly. What story did you make up about x?"

Kids can start to understand reality and fantasy by age three to four but don't fully grasp the difference at that age. At young ages, you might have to really help children with telling stories. Acting out with puppets or drawing pictures can help this process. Using comic strips with thinking and talking bubbles with older kids can also help with this process. With older children, you can remind them: Events are more factual and really happen. Stories happen in our brains / thinking bubbles. Stories involve thoughts, and they only occur in the brain of one person.

Sharing of your own experiences and separating out the story can help create rapport with your kids. The key is to really listen to their answers, both the verbal and the nonverbal information. When you show up without judgment and with an open heart, you'll find that kids are really sharp when it comes to naming their own story. Fantasy and reality with kids can get blurred, so it is important for parents to help kids by asking questions and getting more information about the story. Also remember you get to respect their experience. There is no way you can stop your child from experiencing upset, betrayal, fear, or hurt. But you can give them tools and the support they need to learn how to witness rather than believe their inner stories.

"What do you know is true (what really happened) in this situation?" Again, you can begin teaching children the difference between the truth and a story at an early age. A way to get kids to get to what is true is to have them say what happened. Ask questions about who, what, where, when, and the events and how they played out. Ask the child what they saw, heard, and felt. Make it a game: You can show the extremes of where our minds can go with a story (*Molly is not talking to me* [this really happened] *so Molly doesn't want to be my friend* [this is a thought, a story, something I am telling myself in my mind/brain]) and what other things might be possible (*Molly is not talking to me because she didn't sleep well last night*, or *She got in a fight with her brother*, or *She has a sore throat*). It is good to teach kids how to make guesses about others. It is also really good to teach them to be curious and ask questions if they wonder about things that happen. Then you can explore what is actually true / what actually happened in the situation (*Molly didn't talk to me at lunch* [this is true], *and I felt* _____ [this is the emotion], *and I'm not sure why* [this is a thought]). It is also important for kids to understand there is truth in how they feel but maybe not in the thoughts connected to the feelings related to others or events.

If you have older children, sit down and ask them how they

know if something is a story or if it is truth. How does their body let them know if something is true? What sensations are associated with truth? Where do they feel it? How does it feel? You can help them learn the difference in how they feel when they are telling themselves a lie or telling the truth. Teaching fact and opinion is also good for older kids.

You can also use this exploration of the difference between story and truth as a larger conversation around social media and advertising, which is notorious for showing us only part of the truth in misleading perfect pictures and only the happy moments of life. It is critical that kids understand that media will often make them feel bad about themselves, because they want them to buy the latest product, and that what is shown on social media is never the whole truth about anybody. It is really important for kids to know that things in social media or advertising are based on thoughts/stories/opinions. Help them find real examples of people who can be role models for them in showing the good and the struggles. If your kids are really young, using actual stories from the many great books now available can help them understand the difference between a hurtful story and a healing truth.

The fourth question, for the Intent Chamber, is a foundational one: "What do you want?" Ask your kids how they would like to feel or what is the most important quality they want to bring to the situation they are exploring. This is to help them discover their intent. Talk to them about the difference between wanting someone else to be different versus them taking action based on how they want to feel or be. This is also a great opportunity to talk about the ideas of accepting other people just the way they are, how to make clear boundaries, and learning (without judgment) through making mistakes.

Once they are clear on their word of intent, you can have them write it down on an index card and decorate it, or even write it on their hand to remind them. Then walk them back through the chambers—Truth, Story, and Feeling—to complete the process. It is a good idea to check back in with them the following day to see how they have integrated their experience, what they learned, and if they have any questions.

You know your kids best, so be creative in how you share the chambers with them.

## MENTAL ILLNESS

If you have been diagnosed with a mental illness, such as borderline personality disorder, depression, or schizophrenia, you will want to gather more tools to work with discerning the difference between the truth and stories. Some of the biggest work you will do is around first releasing any shame around your diagnosis. There is still an unfortunate stigma around mental illness that we as a society are in the midst of shifting. Your work is to make this shift inside of yourself so you are freed from the false belief that you are broken and beyond repair. Just like someone who was born with a physical difference like blindness or scoliosis, your brain's function or body condition does not diminish your worth or value as a human. So do the chamber practice around any shame or self-judgment you might be carrying.

You have gifts to share, and your job is to learn about how your brain functions and how to best support yourself. You'll want to really stalk your thoughts and emotions and watch for any signs that your brain chemistry is out of balance. As you learn your own signals and signs, you'll be able to adjust earlier and know when you need to slow down and get clear before you take any action.

The tools of grounding and self-reflection are critical for all of us, and especially so for people with mental challenges. Grounding is a simple practice to connect with the earth through visualization; I usually use the image of a tree rooting into the earth, or a channel of light that connects me to the earth. For more information on grounding, please see chapter 4 of my book *Warrior Goddess Training* (applicable to men and women!).

One helpful thing to do is to create a list of warning signs that you are being compromised by your mind rather than supported. So, for example, you may notice that your depression begins as a negative voice telling you that you are worthless. If you understand the early warning signs, you can take a new action to get support or shift your brain pattern. Or, if you have borderline personality disorder, you may see that whenever you are feeling that you are unloved and unlovable, you should first take several deep breaths and figure out what is actually true before you react.

Many shamanic cultures view what we in the West call *mental illness* as a form of spiritual initiation. From working with people with mental health issues, I've found that the best gift you can give yourself is to read as much as you can from people who are successfully dealing with the same issues as you are. I've included a list of books for different mental challenges below. And please make sure that you are working with a good therapist or coach who has experience with your particular issues. It's not something to be ashamed about; just like someone with a physical struggle, you need an expert who can guide you to navigate in the best way possible for you and your capabilities.

An important note from my friend Chris Curra, who has worked through her own depression and mental health issues:

It is important to know the difference of an emotion—which is an energy that can move if we let it—versus the mental state of anxiety or depression, which produces difficult emotions. Be conscious of what practices alleviate and help heal the neurological wiring of mental illness versus common practices which can contribute to more hardwiring of the illness. Being mindful of things such as "if I don't get enough sleep, it triggers a manic episode" is helpful in determining the best route of self-care. However, sitting in a pure mindfulness meditation observing anxiety can actually be strengthening the anxiety response in your neurons. Other forms of meditation can actually help break up that patterning in the brain.

Chris also shares:

In the past, I had experienced severe depressions. The stories my mind would tell me when I was depressed were only snares to drag me further into the abyss. And though I rarely get depressed now, I will on occasion have a few days of low-level depression. A few winters back, I had been down for a few days when I started to notice other symptoms of depression. Instead of going into the emotion or story (especially the one of fear around how bad things could potentially get), there was a simple truth. *Aha, this is biochemical; I'm experiencing depression.* With the intent to get help for my brain, I contacted a healer who specializes in natural herbal remedies. What she suggested I take worked within a few days to correct my brain chemistry. (Again, this was a very mild depression, and even then, I did not hesitate to ask for help. Having a Warrior Heart does not mean going it all alone or having to suffer through.)

## TRAUMA

If you have experienced physical or sexual abuse, or negative effects due to medical procedures, or if you find yourself experiencing high anxiety, panic attacks, intense rage, depression, hopelessness, or completely disconnecting (disassociating) when you attempt to sit with your feelings as you do the Warrior Heart practice, you may need additional support on your healing journey.

Our individual reactions to life events are complex and unpredictable. Some people come out of very difficult life experiences with more resiliency and capacity. Trauma is not in the event but in the nervous system of the person experiencing the event. So the same event or experience could affect two people in completely different ways (one with resilience and one perceiving the event as traumatic having very negative effects), while others may suffer coping with life, leading them to become more hypersensitive and easily triggered. **Your reaction to past events does not make you a weak or a bad person.** Trauma gets locked in the nervous system of the body, and it takes specific types of guidance to unravel and clear the mental, emotional, and physical effects.

If you know you have PTSD or other trauma-related responses to stimuli, please proceed gently with the Warrior Heart practice. It is best to find someone who specializes in trauma therapy or counseling. I highly recommend finding a somatic- (body-) based therapist. It is critical that you learn specific skills and tools to both avoid retraumatizing yourself and to slowly release the trauma from your body, desensitize/heal your nervous system, and stretch your capacity to sit with intense emotions/thoughts/experiences. You can share the Warrior Heart practice with your therapist or guide and ask them to lead you through the process. This way, they can observe and help you to notice what is happening in the body so that you can regulate your system and stay present in your body.

My experience with trauma, both in myself and with friends and students, is that you must proceed slowly and with great care. This is not a time to try to "power through" your emotions or reactions. Please don't beat yourself up because you cannot let go of a story or you get stuck in a feeling. There are physiological and chemical responses at work, and trying to use the mind to "get over" trauma usually causes people to bypass their emotions and pretend that they are okay. This is a form of self-abandonment that does not lead to healing but to deeper distrust in the body and psyche.

At the end of this appendix is a list of resources if you think you may be having a trauma reaction or if you are a support person for someone with past trauma.

If you are in a relationship with a person who has experienced trauma, listen with great kindness and presence to their experiences and struggles. You don't need to coddle them or walk on eggshells, but you do need to understand that they are dealing with intense physical, chemical, and brain challenges that are not going to be fixed by telling them to "just stop telling yourself the story" or asking them, "Why are you still reacting to that?" People who have experienced trauma need calm presence and love and your faith that they will find the resources and tools to heal.

One of my students, Laura, shared with me while learning the Warrior Heart practice:

> Sometimes the Feeling Chamber was too triggering, and the Story Chamber just sent a part of me spinning. I couldn't get to the truth from that place, and it often

retraumatized me. I've found what helped was skipping the Feeling and Story Chambers and going straight to truth, while using a lot of supportive self-talk. The importance of knowing you are safe and that whatever the trauma is, is not happening now is so, so important.

Orienting to safety has become my many-times-a-day practice. Just knowing you are safe and having your body believe it can really start to change someone's life. Trauma collapses time for sure, so learning to stretch it is the practice for me. It gives time to pause, breathe, and reflect before reacting out of fear. It also gives time to get out of freeze and feel your body, whatever is present. It helps so much to know you are not alone and that others have these experiences. Even as I struggle with my reactions, it helps so much to understand what the body does and acknowledge that I am where I am and I've come so far. I'm getting more and more clear. It is so good to know that the trauma reaction is just a part of me and not the whole.

## Chris: The Warrior Heart Practice for Trauma

We are living in an exciting time for Western neuropsychology where technology is giving us understanding of how trauma affects the nervous system as well as why certain practices (both ancient and recently developed) work to heal trauma and PTSD. I have been fortunate to work with an osteopath and a chiropractor who were well versed in polyvagal theory and did amazing craniosacral work, releasing much of the trauma held in my nervous system.

I also was fortunate to be a student of HeatherAsh when she was first teaching the Warrior Heart practice. I continue to use it frequently for the normal day-to-day triggers as a tool to let emotion move and uncover and transform deep agreements and bring greater presence to my inner world. That said, when dealing with a body that has suffered trauma, self-knowledge, compassion, and intelligence are needed to know what practices will help and when.

I had had a significant session with the osteopath releasing not only the vagus nerve but restrictions in the pelvic floor. Two days later, apparently my cells were ready to release more trauma at a deeper level. Standing in the kitchen just finishing doing my dishes, I suddenly, with no apparent trigger, had a flashback of a childhood trauma. I held on to the edge of the counter as my body completely froze. I was not feeling emotion and had almost no thoughts. I went into the Warrior Heart practice but immediately altered the normal practice. Knowing that reliving memories of trauma can actually retraumatize the nervous system, I immediately shut the door of the Story Chamber—the flashback is the story. I stepped into the Truth Chamber.

Truth: *This is a flashback. It happened in the past. It is not happening now. That is the truth.*

Truth: *I am safe in this moment. I am alone, and the doors of my apartment are locked. In this moment, I am safe.*

I had entered into a witness space, noticing my body still frozen, and more amazing to me was the stillness in my mind.

Then the third truth arose spontaneously: *This is an opportunity for healing.*

I stepped into the Intent Chamber. *My intent is to take care of my body and my nervous system. My intent is to use this moment to heal.*

From there, I started asking the question, *What does my body need now?* For quite a while, it was clear my body needed to stay very still. When finally the body was ready to move, I repeated the question, *What does my body need now to help it heal?* My mind back online, I went through the tool set I have acquired, physical and psychological practices from such resources as Peter Levine, Julie Hendersen, and Rick Hansen, letting my body dictate which ones would work best in each moment. Eventually, reminding myself that the truth was I was safe in the moment, I went outside and leaned into a large tree. I asked it to help to bring my energy body back into my physical body and show me how to ground it into the earth.

On this occasion, by not going to the Feeling and Story Chambers at all and potentially ending up in a victim story or retraumatizing my nervous system or creating emotions that were not present, I was able instead to use the Truth and Intent Chambers as a means of healing and self-love.

**LONG-TERM PHYSICAL ILLNESS**

The Warrior Heart practice can be very useful in unwinding agreements and beliefs the keep us from really listening to what our body needs when we are ill. It can also be used to uncover energetic and mental imbalances or blocks that are contributing to it.

First, use the Warrior Heart practice to clear any shame, blame, or self-judgment around the illness. Explore how you feel about the illness, the story you are telling yourself around the illness, what the truth is, and what your intent is in relation to the illness. Really take time with your intent and make sure it is empowering and feels healing. Then when you go back through the chambers, be creative in how you rewrite your story in relation to your illness. Again, you want the story to feel empowering or peaceful rather than based in judgment or fear. I'm reminded of something Donald Epstein, author of *Healing Myths, Healing Magic,* explained: Healing does not necessarily mean you get better or even that you do not die. Healing is an attitude, a new relationship with yourself that brings peace and love.

For over a decade now, I've struggled with food sensitivities that leave me in pain after eating things like carrots, coconut, garlic, pepper, grains, and about a dozen other random and in-everything substances. I would go through phases of ignoring the discomfort and finding myself getting more and more bloated, inflamed, and unhappy (and eventually sick), and then cutting everything out of my diet that was irritating and finding myself struggling to find things I could eat while I was traveling and losing weight and energy (and eventually getting sick).

When I finally tried the Warrior Heart practice for my symptoms, it did not fix the problem right away. But it gave me a new sense of hope and connection to my body. While I sat in the Feeling Chamber, I recognized that I had been dealing with a sensitive intestinal tract for much longer than I thought: I discovered the same feeling of being overfull and inflamed when I was in college. I sat and listened to my belly. *What are you feeling? What message are you wanting to share with me?* In the Story Chamber, I discovered a story I had created that I was "broken" and could never heal. As I sat in the Truth Chamber, I had a sudden realization: There was an underlying cause to my sensitivities. The story I had created was that once you have food sensitivities, you are going to have to always be dealing with them. I was holding that as the truth. But what if that wasn't true and there was something deeper I hadn't connected to yet? My intent: Get to the root. As I went back through the chambers, I realized I had given up in a way and that I needed to reconnect with my desire to heal again. I felt hopeful and curious.

The next day, I called a healer that I'd been to before, who was notoriously difficult to get in to see. After a week on the waiting list, they found an opening for me. Ten minutes into the session, Dr. Storkon said, "Well, the big thing is that you have a hiatal hernia. That could account for all your symptoms."

Boom. Root solution. He pulled my stomach down out of my diaphragm, showed me how to adjust myself, and cleared me of several food sensitivities. I'm not symptom-free, but I am much more mindful of the importance of sitting up while I eat, eating slowly, and continuing to be mindful of what I am putting in my body and how my body responds.

It may take time to rewrite your story around your illness, so be patient and keep coming back to it. Once you have this new relationship with your intent and story, you can begin to explore the chambers in regard to specific symptoms, how other people are treating you, or even around what your choices are around treatment and support. Doing the Warrior Heart practice will help you to get the story out of the way so you can gain access to the wisdom of your body and heart to help guide you forward.

More specific examples and ways to use the Warrior Heart

practice will be available in the upcoming *Warrior Heart Practice Companion Guide*.

## Resources for Working with Mental Illness

*The Buddha & the Borderline* by Kiera Van Gelder
*The Dialectical Behavior Therapy Skills Workbook* by Matthew McKay
*The Collected Schizophrenias* by Esmé Weijun Wang
*Accessing the Healing Power of the Vagus Nerve* by Stanley Rosenberg
*Spiritual Emergency* by Stanislav Grof
*Feeling Good: The New Mood Therapy* by David D. Burns
Uplift   (https://upliftconnect.com/shamanic-view-of -mental-health)

## Resources for Working with Trauma

*Waking the Tiger* by Peter A. Levine
*In an Unspoken Voice* by Peter A. Levine
*Trauma Through a Child's Eyes* by Peter A. Levine and Maggie Kline
*The Body Keeps the Score* by Bessel van der Kolk
*Getting Past Your Past* by Francine Shapiro
*Complex PTSD: From Surviving to Thriving* by Pete Walker
Somatic Experiencing Trauma Institute (https:// traumahealing.org)

# Acknowledgments

There have been many champions for this book, but none more dedicated, supportive, and tenacious than my agent, Anne Marie O'Farrell. I originally met Anne Marie when I was working for Amber-Allen Publishing in the early 2000s; she was the agent for many of our books. Almost fifteen years later I sent her the first rough draft of a book I was working on and after reading it she told me, "This is not it, but there is something here. I do want to work with you." And work with me she did: Anne Marie guided me over the next six years to refine and re-refine my proposal. She hung in with me as I went through huge life upheavals and didn't work on the book for years; she was patient as I put this project on hold and wrote *Warrior Goddess Training*; she stayed open as I evolved and the Warrior Heart practice evolved into what you are holding in your hands today. I had asked to find an agent who saw the potential in me and could help me bring it out and into the world, and Anne Marie did this and so much more. I'm so grateful for your friendship, love, fierce determination, and your Warrior Heart, Anne Marie.

Huge gratitude to my publisher, Joel Fotinos, another incredible Warrior of the Heart whose enthusiasm and belief in this book made it a joy to finish the final manuscript. Thanks to the entire team at St. Martin's for the creativity you have brought to the entire process of midwifing *The Warrior Heart Practice*. And a big hug and blessings to Brooke Kaye, who always has my back in regard to editing and proofing my writing with her clear eye. Your questions always help me to share what I meant to say, which is not always what comes out the first try.

And many blessings to the people I lovingly call my "trees." As an author who is on the road most of the time, I find refuge in the beloveds in my life who are well rooted and always there to extend their love, great conversation, and nourishing meals. Special gratitude to Perdita Finn and Clark Strand for many long hikes, late-night talks, sharing your expertise of the publishing world and your love of writing, and for the companionship I've found in the Way of the Rose community. To my New York trees—Matthew Stillman, Sarika Jain, and Krishan Patel—thank you for holding me so beautifully during my year living in your neighborhood in Harlem and beyond; what a gift. To my main Santa Fe trees: Franklin Cunico, I'm so blessed to have you in my life again. Thank you for the dancing, the laughter, dreaming and working the land with me, for all the adventures, and for the feeding and caring of Shima. You are a blessing. Gini Gentry, gratitude for our friendship, my wonderful home in the sun-drenched rocks of your land in Cerrillos, New Mexico, which I visit sporadically, and early morning coffee served with inspiration. To my many deep-rooted Northern California trees: You know who you are. I love you. Big gratitude to

Sarah Marshank (Thelma! Or are you Louise?) for teaching and holding and exploring with me as we both developed our own forms of getting to the truth during a year-long program we taught together in Austin, Texas. While I birthed the Warrior Goddess practice, she birthed Selfistry, so I consider them best friend practices that grew up together and inspired and informed each other. Yes! And special unbounded blessings to Kevin Braheny Fortune, who has been my companion in the power of radical truth-telling, fierce loving, and being fully present in the good times and the hard times for over two decades. You are a treasure in my life.

# Index

# The Warrior Heart Practice Sheet

**Start with a situation that is challenging or upsetting.** Begin with the **Feeling Chamber**, answering the questions and writing out what you are feeling without editing or trying to understand. Sit and simply be with your feelings for a moment. Then move on to the **Story Chamber**. Again, write without editing. Answer the questions, being curious about your story and what you think about the situation. Next, explore the **Truth Chamber**. Answer the questions, remembering the truth is simple! Then in the **Intent Chamber** pick one main word for your intent and write it down. Now flip the page and circle back through the Chambers.

---

**FEELING**

What am I feeling? • How does it affect my physical body? • Where do I feel closed and where do I feel open?

---

**STORY**

What am I telling myself? • What words have I woven together? • What old agreements/rules are embedded in my story?

---

**TRUTH**

What is an ultimate truth right now? • What is true about this situation? • What do I wish were true versus what is actually a fact?

---

**INTENT**

What do I actually want in this situation? • Where do I want to put my focus? • Pick **one word** for your intent.

---

Now that you have clarified your Intent, you circle back through the Chambers to gain new insights and awareness. This time focus on the **Intent Chamber**. Rewrite your word in bold letters, claiming your Intent. Now revisit the **Truth Chamber**. Write down any new truths you perceive. With new willingness and spaciousness, step back into the **Story Chamber**. How can you perceive your story differently? Rewrite and explore how to integrate your Intent and the Truth to transform your experience of the Story. Even if the story itself remains a difficult one, your relationship to the story changes from victimization or judgment to power and curiosity. End in the **Feeling Chamber**.

---

**INTENT**

Write your intent again, and take a moment to close your eyes and notice what your intent feels like in your body.

---

**TRUTH**

Imagine you are holding hands with your Intent, and now you are going to hold hands with the Truth. What other truths do you see?

---

**STORY**

How can you perceive your story differently now that you are holding hands with your intent and truth? What can you shift?

---

**FEELINGS**

Always end with being in your feelings. How do you feel? Take a breath and acknowledge what is happening in your body now.

---